MONEY

TO LAST A LIFETIME

MONEY

TO LAST A LIFETIME

The Road to a Comfortable Retirement and Beyond

Lois Fishman, CFP

ODYSSEY
Publications, LLC

Odyssey Publications, LLC
Rockville, Maryland

MONEY to Last a Lifetime:
The Road to a Comfortable Retirement and Beyond

ISBN 0-9741548-0-6
Library of Congress No. 2003097393

Publisher
Odyssey Publications, LLC
16605 Bethayres Rd.
Rockville, Maryland 20855
Telephone (301) 330-9455
Facsimile (301) 330-2641
Email: fishman@erols.com
Website: www.moneytolastalifetime.com

Securities offered through
H. Beck, Inc.
Member NASD/SIPC
11140 Rockville Pike
4th Floor
Rockville, Maryland 20852
(301) 468-0100

Cover photo of Lois Fishman by Danny Peck of PeckStudios.net

Manufactured in the United States of America on acid-free paper.

To my clients,
from whom I have learned more than
any textbook could have taught me.

Contents

Preface

Empowerment, enlightenment, control, independence; these are the four words that should describe your relationship with money. It is how you relate to your money that sets you apart from other people. In order to achieve your goals and reach financial independence, you must first understand your finances and how your money works. You must gain the knowledge that is necessary so that you can make smart decisions along the way and become disciplined enough to stick with those decisions. You must be able to use this knowledge so that you are making decisions based on facts not emotions. We have all seen just how emotional the markets can be but you should not make decisions about your future strictly based on your emotions.

Blindly delegating the responsibility of money management to a spouse or other family member, a friend or even a professional is not the way to go. Working with a professional does not relieve you of your responsibilities. While you may depend on a professional planner to bring information to the table, provide objectivity, and support, you must take control by educating yourself. You must be able to understand those recommendations made by a professional and be able to ask the right questions and not just accept their recommendations as gospel. Blindly delegating the responsibility only sets you up for failure and shock when things do not go as you had hoped. In addition if you are totally dependent on a spouse or friend for this service, what would happen if they died unexpectedly or became seriously ill and could no longer play this role. How would you cope? Over the years, I have seen the fear and confusion that results from this scenario.

It is your money and you need to take the ultimate responsibility for it. I truly believe that working with a professional is the very best way to go to get objectivity and guidance. However, unless you are in the know, you can't truly judge if the advice you are getting is in your best interests or whether the advice is appropriate given your situation. Being in the know also helps your advisor help you. It makes it easier to discuss the various nuances when the planner knows that the client fully understands them and their possible consequences.

Congratulations! You have taken the first step toward developing that relationship with your finances. By working through this manual, you will develop an intimate knowledge of the assets you own and how they relate to each other. You can expect to gain a broader vocabulary to include some of the buzz words of the industry making it more enjoyable to pick up the financial pages of your newspaper or even to begin reading some of the financial publications available to you. You will have a better understanding of your cash flow and how to get ahead of it. You will develop strategies and learn techniques to pass on your assets and protect them from long-term healthcare risks. The stress level you experience now as it relates to your finances should drop dramatically and you might experience some euphoria over your new feelings of empowerment and control.

While this is an exciting venture for you, don't expect it to be an easy one. As in everything worthwhile, this will take time and effort on your part. You can expect to spend several hours gathering the proper documents and then some more analyzing the information you have found. You have been provided with worksheets and charts to follow and fill in. Take your time and digest the information as you go. Try to set a time and place for this activity so that you are consistent in working this through in a timely fashion. Follow the chapters in the order they are arranged since each section is built upon what is learned in the section before. Actually, the information that you will be gathering is used over and over in various ways to analyze ways in which you can make your finances more cohesive.

This book is divided into three sections covering Basic Money Management, Investing for Success, and Estate Planning. Each manual is further subdivided into topics and "lessons." You will be guided though various exercises that will make these materials very personalized and can serve as a resource for many years to come. You should add to it from time to time and reproduce some of the worksheets for your use in the future.

The supplies you will need are as follows:

Pencils, pens calculator;

Three ring binder, separators;

Small file box or cabinet;

Hanging files;

Employee benefit book/recent statements;

Recent pension and 401k statements;

A copy of your will, trust, etc.;

Copies of insurance policies *(life, health, disability, homeowners, tenant, car, long term care, etc.)*;

Most recent tax return; and

Statements from your banks, mutual funds, brokerage accounts.

So let's approach this with a positive state of mind and with great conviction. By the end you will be rewarded with greater knowledge, increased power, more confidence and less stress. Let's get started!

Acknowledgments

Over the many months it took to write this book, many people gave freely of their time and expertise in helping me. They also provided much encouragement along the way. I want to thank Joseph Jacques, CPA, Robert Bender, CPA, Sarah Flynn, friend and editor, and Norman Handler, Attorney-at-Law, for their insights and marketing ideas.

I want to specially thank Timothy E. Hall for having taken a great deal of time away from his busy schedule to thoroughly edit and critique this book in great detail and for giving me the confidence to actually get it published.

I want to thank my family for their support and patience during the time it took to create this.

Part One

Basic Money Management

In **Part One** you will learn **Basic Money Management**

We will kick off this exercise with some advice relative to choosing a financial planner and making them a part of your financial future. We will walk you through the process of understanding the profession and how it operates. You will always be in the driver's seat with your finances but will need various tools to move smoothly.

This will be followed by the development of a system to get organized. No longer will your papers and documents be scattered. Then you will learn about setting budgets, balancing your checkbooks, and managing cash flow.

Once you have a handle on all this, we will walk you through your tax return so you can make the connection between those forms and your personal finances.

From there you will create a balance sheet that we will use again and again through the rest of the book. Take the time to do the exercises. Once you are done, the rest is maintenance. Once you are done, you will be relieved knowing where everything is.

Finally, but not least importantly, is the setting of goals. You will need to design your future plans around them. Once we know where we are going, it is easy to figure out how to get there. They will guide our decisions about investments, insurance and estate planning as we move through Part Two and Part Three.

Got your supplies? Let's get going!

Why You Need A Financial Advisor

1

The process of learning is never-ending. Therefore, everyone needs to be open to new ideas and be *willing* to learn. In current times, we are inundated with so many bits of information relative to our finances. We read the newspapers, listen to the TV with more channels than we ever thought possible, read periodicals and surf the Internet. So many ***sources***; so much advice! Each source has "the" answer to your problems and each makes a good case for itself. There are no advertisements for products that claim to be the worst and none that claim to be mediocre. They all say they are the "best".

Yet, we all know that there are some real dogs out there as well as some really bad advice.

How Is a Person to Know?

- *What should be accepted and what should be discarded?*
- *What will work for them, given their own unique circumstances, and what won't?*
- *How the options presented stack up against each other?*
- *How to keep current with changes in investments as time goes by?*
- *How to keep up with the myriad of tax law changes and updates that are constantly being created?*
- *How to keep up with new planning strategies and opportunities on the horizon?*

Being on top of things requires more time than most people are willing to devote. A professional does nothing else. Following these issues is their full time job!

Even if you fancy yourself to be a "do-it-yourselfer," it is wise to listen to others. You might learn something. Left on one's own, a person is more likely to succumb to the emotions of "greed and fear".

It is hard to remain objective with your own money.

Let's look back to the Crash of 1987. Many investors pulled out for fear of losing more. They liquidated, took their losses and retreated to "safer" ground. Those who stayed in, however, had enjoyed the biggest run up in stock prices in history. At the time, many studies were done and it was found that more of the investors that pulled out did not work with an advisor and many that stayed in did. It is hard to remain objective with your own money. Financial advisors are good sounding boards for even the most sophisticated person. They lend objectivity when it is needed. A financial advisor is someone that can guide you through the maze and help you make the best choices given the options in front of you.

Now is the time to begin doing your homework.

Having someone on board who you can trust can be a source of comfort in times of transition or crisis. For example, if a couple develops a relationship with a planner and one spouse becomes ill or dies, the other spouse does not need to panic but rather can just pick up the phone and call. In addition, when a financial issue arises, as it does in all of our lives from time to time, it is comforting to be able to pick up the phone and get help. Times of crisis are not the time to begin doing your homework and search for an advisor. The ***time*** is now!

Choosing Your Financial Advisor

The results of your search can have a great impact on your financial future. The financial advisor you choose should be able to guide you towards sound financial decisions based on a deep understanding of your goals and dreams and ability to tolerate risk. That person must become your 'financial mentor'.

The financial advisor you choose should be independent. This means that they either are self-employed or employed within a group of independent advisors. By independent, I mean not being affiliated with any particular investment or insurance company, which by their very nature may encourage the sales of proprietary products. After a thorough analysis you will want your advisor to select strategies and /or products that are in *your* best interest. An independent advisor should search the marketplace to find the correct strategies and products to suit your *individual* needs, goals and temperament.

The advisor you choose should come with recommendations from satisfied clients. Don't be shy about asking for references. Then call them and interview them.

Choose an independent advisor.

Questions You Should Ask

- *Has the advisor considered their **needs** when making recommendations?*
- *Has the advisor exhibited a high sense of **integrity** in their dealings?*
- *Has the advisor been **easy** to talk to?*
- *Does the advisor **listen** more than talk?*
- *Has the advisor been **available** to them on short notice?*
- *What are the advisor's greatest **strengths**? **Weaknesses**?*

There are various ways to find a financial planner that is right for you.

Perhaps the best way is through a referral from a trusted friend or relative. You can also ask for a referral from your CPA or attorney. If you do not have a ready source for referrals, call the local chapter of the Financial Planning Association and they will be able to give you the names of four or five planners in your area. This will not be an endorsement of their ability but rather a place to start. Treat these leads as you would any new person and interview them. Look for those who offer a free preliminary consultation. Take some financial planning courses. Not only will you learn more about

Referrals give you a place to start.

the field but also the instructors can be good leads. (You will be able to get a sense of whether you like them in a low-key environment). If all else fails, there is always the *Yellow Pages*.

Hire someone with solid credentials.

Education, credentials, experience and reputation all count.

The planner you hire should have certain basic qualifications. The most recognized credentials are Certified Financial Planner (CFP) and Chartered Financial Consultant (ChFC). Different institutions issue these certifications, but for all intents and purposes, they are equal in scope. Membership in their professional societies is preferable. In addition, look for someone who has experience in the areas in which you need help. Formal textbook education does not teach a professional everything. Much of what is learned is by experience working with a wide variety of clients. Look for an experienced professional. Finally, find out if the planner is active in the community and try to find out something about his/her reputation.

Learn how the planner is compensated.

There are three categories of compensation. There is the commission only, fee only or a combination of fee and commission. Remember there is a potential for conflict of interest with all three and one way to minimize it is to work with someone who has a high degree of integrity. Let's look at the differences:

Has a product to sell you.

1. **The *commission only*** planner is usually the insurance agent or stockbroker. In order for them to earn a living, they must sell something. In many cases, they have specific products to sell and are looking for customers to buy. Often, the process of financial planning, to find out what matters to you, is missing because it becomes time consuming with no promise of a sale in the near future. This is not to imply that commission salespeople do not have your best interests at heart. Many folks who operate in this area are highly competent and professional and will take the necessary time to get to know you. This is where interviewing and getting references come into play.

Only plans, doesn't implement.

2. **The *fee only*** planner consults with you and takes you through the process of looking at goals and expectations and then projects a strategy for your financial well being. A benefit is their objectivity since they have nothing to sell but their knowledge and time. Typically, the fees will be higher than a fee and commission planner and you will be billed for time spent including phone calls, etc. When their work is done, you will have to begin all over again with other financial professionals in order to implement the plan. Once the planning work is done, the fee only planner has no incentive to motivate you to implement. So you are on your own here. The process of monitoring your assets, once purchased elsewhere, may be possible with this planner but you will need to inquire as to the availability of services and additional costs. Unless you are able to implement on your own, with your own study and research, you will be paying a commission to someone else so that they can sell you the products you need. On the other hand, if you go through the process of having a financial plan prepared and do not implement, you have wasted the funds you've already spent.

3. **The *fee and commission*** mode of compensation is the most common. This type of planner will look at your goals and work through a plan. They will charge you a fee for the development of the plan and earn a commission when you purchase products. Based on this information, the planner will recommend strategies to accomplish your goals. In addition, the planner should try to coordinate all aspects of the process and your finances to establish a well-rounded program. By going through this process, the planner will know all there is to know about you so that when the time comes for implementation, then he/she should be able to sift through the multitude of products to find those that are suitable for you. You should work with an independent planner who is not under firm-mandated sales or product quotas. Because the planner has multiple sources of income, this type of planner usually can keep the fees lower. Because of this, you can be sure that the planner is motivated to get you to implement.

Plans, implements and has products available.

In any case, the planner should be an individual or be associated with a company that is either registered with the Securities and Exchange Commission or the states in which he/she operates. If they are, they are required to provide you, both initially and every year thereafter, with a copy of Part II of their ADV *(This is a disclosure form filed with either the Securities and Exchange Commission or the State the planner is practicing in or both. It will disclose their educational and work background, give details relative to how they operate and get paid and detail about any disciplinary actions that may have been taken against them).* If the person you are interviewing is referring to themselves as a financial planner and charges fees for their services, they are obliged by law to offer this to you. If they refuse, run, don't walk, and move on to the next candidate.

Be aware of your rights!

Remember to research the planner, interview and then go with the planner that made you feel the most comfortable. There should be a good chemistry between you and the advisor. You need to feel comfortable working with that person since you may be developing a life long relationship with them. You should consider that person a partner in your plans for the future.

Feel comfortable with the person you choose.

When you appear for the first consultation you need to be prepared. Often the first meeting is at no cost, but either way, you want to spend your time productively. Bring with you statements from your investments, pension plans etc. It would be helpful for you to bring the completed worksheets from this book. After the first meeting, you should be made aware of the work that planner will be doing for you and what it will cost. Although the process' vary from planner to planner, typically you will be returning for a fact finding meeting and then again one or more times for the presentation of the plan by the planner.

Be prepared to participate.

Financial Planner Interview

Don't be shy — ask these questions.

1. Name of planner: ______________________________
2. Planner's credentials:

   ____

   ____

3. Number of years in practice: ______________
4. Is planner independent? ______________
5. Does planner work for a company that sells its own products? ______________
6. Compensation type: ______________
7. Does planner have a minimum account size? ______________
8. Profile of planner's typical client:

   ____

   ____

9. Planner's specialty: ______________
10. Have you reviewed the planner's ADV form? ______________
11. Client referrals:

    Name: ______________________ Phone ______________

    Name: ______________________ Phone ______________

    Name: ______________________ Phone ______________

12. General impressions about this planner:

    Do I have confidence in this person?

    Do I feel that this person is concerned about what is in my best interest?

Getting Yourself Organized | 2

Over the years, I have found that this is a most difficult challenge for many people. Yet, once accomplished, it produces the greatest sense of achievement and satisfaction.

One of the worst cases of disorganization that I have run into involves the story of a son who was charged with being the executor of his father's estate. Dad had passed away, and Mom had no idea where any of the family accounts or investments were. She never took an interest in the family finances, having had enough to enjoy a comfortable lifestyle. The son had no idea where to begin, so he started to write letters to anyone who sent any financially oriented information to the house. The son's curiosity was again piqued when he went to clean out his father's fishing cabin only to find over a **MILLION DOLLARS** in stock certificates in a bin next to the fireplace. Mom had no idea about any of this. The family is unsure that they will ever locate all the assets that might have existed. Nor do they have a way to bring closure to these issues.

Know about all your family assets.

Let's Make Things Better for You and Your Family!

You will need some basic supplies. Buy a three-ring binder and enough dividers so that each investment account is separate. Also, you will need either a file box or a cabinet with a box of files to label later.

Gather your supplies.

Anyone who has any investments at all is too familiar with the mounds of paper and statements that arrive in the mail. Even if you are just starting out and only have a 401k, they too send statements. So, a beginner would have this and bank statements to organize.

Step One: Take out your three-ring binder and dividers. Gather all your statements (bank, brokerage, pension, etc.). Set up a divider for each and every investment, brokerage accounts, IRA etc. Label each tab. Then begin to sort out all the statements you have from each and set them in piles. Once you have them divided up, sort each individual category by date with the earliest statement on the bottom and the most recent on the top. Three hole punch the statements and insert them in the binder. You should keep the monthly statements but then discard them as the new ones come in **if** they indicate cumulative reporting. This means that each subsequent statement holds the prior months activities as to purchases, sales, dividends and capital gains. Also, keep year-end statements to have a record of dividend reinvestments for later tax needs if you should choose to sell the investment or just to do tax planning. Keep your year-end statements indefinitely. If your year-end statement has a complete record of the year's activity, throw out the monthly and quarterly statements you may have kept.

Keep all year-end statements for as long as you own the asset.

Make sure you also have a tab for your checking account statements (put cancelled checks in a box by month and save for three years), savings and money markets. Keep all monthly statements from these sources. If, at year end, those sections get bulky you may want to either get a larger binder or a second one.

Now you have a system for all those statements as they arrive. Don't accumulate a pile. It is easier to file them in the binder as they arrive. To the front of the binder keep your balance sheets and any other review reports you might acquire relative to the portfolio.

Your documents and other records.

Step Two: Now you will need the file folders and your file box or cabinet. Let's look at those important documents you may have. Rather than initiate a search every time a document is needed, it is vital to keep all of them together and organized as well. We will use your folders to accumulate those documents and bits of information that could become invaluable to your and your family. If you are married, you may want to keep separate folders for each spouse. Set up a separate file to hold each of the following items:

a. **Bank Accounts**: List all accounts, name of bank, title of accounts, addresses of banks and phone numbers as well as a contact.

b. **Brokerage Accounts:** List broker's name, address and phone number. Also, include in their file a list of all mutual fund companies with whom you do business along with account numbers, addresses and phone numbers. Also list your limited partnership interests and other business or investment activities.

c. **Creditors:** To whom do you write checks every month? List all accounts including utilities, credit cards, insurances and cable with addresses and phone numbers. If you became ill and someone else needed to take this over for a while, they will need to pay all of your bills. *How can they if they don't know what they are?*

d. **Insurance Policies:** Keep all your coverages together. Keep all policies for life insurance, health insurance, long-term care, auto and homeowners insurance in this file. You may want to list the companies, their policy numbers and other basic information i.e. death benefits (all this information should be on the front page of the policy) and put this list in the safe deposit box. Remember that the policies are replaceable at no cost if lost or damaged.

e. **Document File:** This includes birth certificates, death certificates, marriage certificates, divorce decrees, military records, social security cards, passports, pre and postnuptial agreements, etc.

f. **Tax Return File:** You should include copies of the last three years tax returns and their supporting documents.

g. **Safe Deposit Box:** Note the location of the box/boxes and an extra key. Remember that to get into your safe deposit box you must sign and show ID. So don't worry about theft. However, if they should get lost or stolen, report it immediately to the bank.

This is worth the effort you are making here!

h. **Ownership File:** A file should be set up for copies of deeds and notes for property such as real estate and cars. Originals can be put in the safe deposit box. This file can also hold copies of closing statements and any other financial description of the property.

i. **Advisors:** Set up a file listing all your current advisors (accountants, lawyers, brokers, insurance agents, and financial planners). Also, include a list of your medical doctors and their respective specialties. For all, list names, addresses and phone numbers. Should you become incapacitated, your spouse/children need to know whom to contact.

j. **Balance Sheet:** A copy of your most recent balance sheet should be included each year. We will take you through a process to develop one on your own.

Once these projects are completed, you are ready to take on the rest of your financial management. Adhering to this process should help you remain organized. There is an old saying "a place for everything and everything in its place. " This is one of the golden rules for your finances.

A job well done.

Remaining organized is a challenge for many people. With personal commitments involving family and other activities and with business obligations and travel, most of us are happy if we just don't forget our appointments. This process requires discipline and habit. Once the habit is established, you will find it very comforting.

3 Where Does All the Money Go?

Bill paying is not fun. It is usually the constant reminder of our lack of disposable income that is the most frustrating. Most people ask, *"Where does my money go? I should be able to do more with what I have, but it seems to flow right through my fingers and there is never anything left. What I try to save goes too. Where does it all go?"* **Does this sound familiar?** No matter how high the income, it seems like a constant issue.

Budget planning is a deliberate process that takes some time and commitment. We all know the phrase "no pain, no gain". Is your financial future worth it? If for no other reason, is stress reduction worth the effort?

We Will Help You Make It as Easy as It Can Be.

If you do not have a computer, don't fret. We have included, in the appendix of this workbook, spreadsheets in hard copy that can be reproduced and relabeled to fit any month of the year. Categories can be added or deleted to match your personal household budget.

Be committed!

This is a family event so if you have a spouse or significant other whose money is commingled with yours, this is a project for the two of you and both of you need to be equally committed. This is also an educational exercise. It is not meant to spy on each other's expenditures. Rather, it is to see where all the dollars go and then "together" re-prioritize your spending habits.

Let's Treasure Hunt Together!

Step 1: Take a stand and make a commitment to this project.

Pick a month to start. No time is better than the present. It is usually better, just for simplicity, to start at the first of any month so you get a full month's expenses under that microscope. Avoid December since it is a month that is full with extraordinary expenses due to the holidays. Set aside a time of day to devote to the project. You will need no more than 5 or 10 minutes on a daily basis and perhaps a half-hour at the end of the month to analyze your results. For most of us time is our most precious commodity and so you will want to do this when you are least likely to forget. Perhaps, right before bedtime or right after dinner. Make it a habit. *Many say it takes approximately 30 days to establish a new habit.*

Step 2: Gather all you will need in one area so that you don't have to hunt for your supplies each time you make an entry.

For those of you doing this by hand, it means having your worksheets together, a pencil and a calculator (the $5 version is fine) all handy. The more you have to do to get organized, the less will be your chances of success. For those of you with a computer, it will be easier to be prepared to do the work. Both spouses must participate openly and honestly for this to work.

Be consistent.

Step 3: Keep receipts for every purchase at least until you enter them.

Do this daily so you can reconstruct your day and your out-of-pocket expenses. And YES, you need to account for that candy bar at the train station and the daily cost of that ticket. Yes, you will need to account for the quarter to buy the paper out of the machine and that burger for lunch. The latte at Starbucks counts as well. You need to be serious about this. Consider this financial fitness training.

Get in shape!

Step 4: Figure out the amount of cash that actually comes into your household every month.

This includes your net paycheck, pension check, Social Security check, and investment income received in the mailbox rather than being reinvested or trust income. Be sure to include both incomes and any income from part time or hobby endeavors. Add back any amounts you automatically send to the credit union or money market. *You know, the amount you try to save but keep dipping into when things are tight.* Now, we are not recommending not trying to save. It's just that what is to be considered true savings should never be touched for living expenses and should be allowed to

Account for your cash.

accumulate. After this exercise, you will figure out just how much that can be, given your family expenses. Ultimately, you will be able to roughly calculate how much needs to be deducted for tax so that you don't lend money to Uncle Sam during the year only to get it back without interest next April 15th.

Step 5: You need to see where the money goes.

A daily habit.

First, you will use the sheets with daily columns (see Appendix). We have provided you with standard categories in the appendix. If you have unique ones for your family, then add the categories in the free lines at the bottom. Each day, you will need to input what you spent in each of those categories. If you and your spouse choose different times of day to do this, then copy the page and you will need to combine them at months end. Do what works with the least amount of effort. Do not hold back; you must report *all* expenses. Just report the amounts spent and don't chastise each other or try to make corrections in your spending habits until month's end. Remember, that one spouse may spend what seems too much on clothes while the other may eat out too often. At the end of the day, the expenses must be less than the income. You will have a chance to re-prioritize your spending patterns later in the process. *If you charge anything, credit the item purchased to the appropriate category.* We will account for interest later. *After these exercises, you should be able to develop a plan to get rid of that credit card debt and its upwards of 22%+ interest forever.*

Step 6: At the end of the month, (yes on that last day; don't put it off) add up the amounts spent by yourself and your spouse in each and every category.

Tally your entries.

By now, you will have paid your bills and you have excess cash or not. Transpose the totals to the BUDGET page. This is the one that has two columns for every month of the year. Put your totals in the actual column and category for the month you have just completed.

Step 7: This is the step of most significance: Priority time.

Now is when you look at the amounts spent and determine which expenditures are appropriate and which are questionable. You'll be surprised at the results here. Very often it is the loose change in your pocket that kills the budget. Do you see areas of expenditures that are way out of line? From day to day, a dollar here and $5 there does not seem like a lot but by month's end it could add up.

Here is where you can make a difference.

Hot spots to look for are lunches out and impulsive shopping. Remember *what we are aiming for is deliberate and predictable spending habits.* Now, if you have dollars left at the end of the month over and above your spending habits then you have little to worry about. However, for many, this is not the case. There are many fallacies we have come to believe. For example, purchase goods on sale and save money. If we use a charge card to take advantage of a 20% off sale and take a year to pay it off at 20% interest, what have we really saved? A similar fallacy is deliberately shrinking your cash flow by not properly withholding for tax. The theory is that it becomes forced savings and your tax refund will be used to pay off accumulated bills. However, the IRS gives you no interest and if you spent the money as earned to keep the bills under control, you probably wouldn't have accumulated those bills.

Spend money deliberately, predictably and consistently.

Some questions you may want to ask yourself at this time are: Did you really need all that you purchased last month? Might a bulk purchase be more cost effective? Will you really wear the clothes you just bought? Do you eat out because you enjoy it or are you just too tired after work to cook? Might you cook meals in advance and save money? Can you brown bag it for lunch even a couple times a week? Look for those cash saving strategies that will be easy to accomplish but yet not destroy your lifestyle.

Step 8: Let's understand the budget column now.

At each row, enter an amount that you feel is more appropriate for the next month. Enter it in the next month's budget column. For example, if you are working with the amounts spent in September actual column, put the proposed budgeted amount in the Budget column for October. September, being the first month you are working in, will not have an entry for Budget. *Next month you will be able to see how you have done by comparing the end of October actual expenditures with the Budgeted amount you just entered.* This allows you to readjust the budget every month based on cycles in the year. For example, during holiday time in December, your budget for gifts may go way up but to compensate, you may need to reduce your expenditures in other areas. Or you may choose to budget a set amount for gifts each and every month during the year so that the funds will be there in December when you go shopping. You may choose to set an amount aside each month for those large fixed expenses that show up periodically.

Anticipate your needs to the extent possible.

Step 9: You should continue to repeat this process for at least six months.

Others will want to continue for an indefinite period. It depends on how much control you want to have over your spending habits. Within the first three months you should see significant improvements in cash flow if you are making the right decisions about your spending habits. If you do not see significant changes in your spending habits you will need to repeat Step 7. Repeat it as often as you need until you feel successful.

Create new habits.

We put an emphasis on this exercise to help you become more disciplined in your spending and savings habits. The better control you have over your cash flow the more effective your planning efforts will become. Greater knowledge and cash flow will create greater opportunities for you to invest. After all, the main reason any of you are taking on this effort is so that you can ultimately retire more comfortably and be able to afford the lifestyle that you have dreamed of. As you work your way through this course, begin thinking about just what money means to you.

Several Items to Keep in Mind

- Items purchased with charge accounts are accounted for as 'today' purchases. Payments to charge accounts are in an expense category called debt reduction. This assumes that from here forward you will not add to the debt balance. Going forward, any new charges should be made in amounts that are accounted for in the budget in advance so that you will be able to pay them off at the end of the month. You can assume that once your debts are paid off you will have an increase in your cash flow.
- You should begin to map out on the annual monthly spreadsheet expenditures that occur periodically i.e. quarterly water bill, insurance due quarterly or annually, tax payments etc. Then divide the totals by 12 and set aside money each month to cover them. We recommend that you put these *"escrowed"* funds into a savings account and draw from the account the amounts needed to cover those bills as they come due.
- You could also escrow funds throughout the year for holiday gifts, birthdays, and vacations. This will help you avoid those nasty charge account bills that come a month after the event.
- Plan your cash needs in advance so that you can minimize your visits to the ATM machine. Each withdrawal can cost from a dollar and a half to several dollars per visit and this can add up if you make several visits during the month for small amounts of cash. Be sure to enter the withdrawals and their associated fees in your check register. With your new power derived from a planned budget you should be able to pare down to one visit a week.
- Try to follow sales and discounts for the merchandise you are buying. There are seasons for sales and usually the merchandise is the same but at lower prices. But pay cash or pay off the charge within 30 days to avoid finance charges
- After you pare down the expenses to a comfortable level, add up what is left. This is the amount you should be able to save. This can become the true savings that will allow you to move forward to financial independence. Once money is designated "savings" it should be held sacred and barring a true emergency, should not be touched.

What Are Your Income Needs and Are You Meeting Them?

1. Annual income needs (from Budget Exercise): ________________

2. Income Sources: (List both spouses separately)

Pensions	________	________
Social Security	________	________
Work	________	________
Investments	________	________
Other	________	________

3. Total income from all sources: ________________

4. Surplus / Deficit (1 – 3): ________________

If you have a surplus, then you have the opportunity to begin to save and invest. If you are already in that process, then you may increase the allocations.

On the other hand, if you have a deficit, then you need to re-examine your expenditures. You can also look into increasing the yields on your investments and, thereby, increasing cash flow. This could mean taking on additional risk, so before you do this you should carefully evaluate your risk tolerance levels. You may also consider part-time employment to supplement your needs.

4 Your Balance Sheet

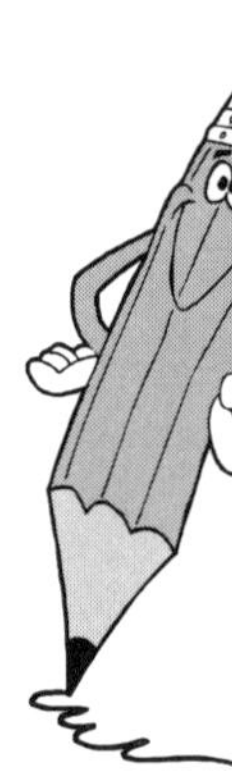

Now we can look at our assets and see what we are truly worth. For the purpose of this exercise, we are looking at all your assets, whether they be investments or personal assets. We will use this completed Balance Sheet again in the Investment Sections, as well as in Part III, when we discuss Estate Planning. So be sure to list everything you own. Make a note of how it is owned (joint, individual husband or wife, pension, IRA, joint with child, trust, custodial).

Remember, a Balance Sheet is a snapshot of your finances on any given day. The values change over time for various reasons. You hopefully make them grow by accumulation of additional assets and they also can grow in value due to appreciation. They can shrink because you spent some of it, sold some of it, or it just goes down in value.

We recommend that you revalue your assets quarterly so that you can see the changes and act if you need to.

Take out your three-ring binders and list your investments according to the categories in the worksheet on the next page. You might need to refer to information in your files for other personal assets. Be as exact as you can.

In today's economy, you might want to research the values of your real estate, since they could be worth more than you think. You can get information from recent sales in your neighborhood or from a Realtor. Jewelry, and other collectibles, should be appraised from time to time for insurance purposes, as well. Now might be a good time to catch up on such activities.

Let's begin!

Now We Can Create a Balance Sheet

ASSETS

Checking / Savings / Life Insurance Cash Values / Annuities

1. ____________________
2. ____________________
3. ____________________
4. ____________________
5. ____________________

Includes rates of interest.

Stocks / Mutual Funds

	Name	Number of Shares	Current Price	Current Value	Cost* Basis
1.					
2.					
3.					
4.					
5.					
6.					

Do your research.

Bonds / T-bills / Other

1. ____________________
2. ____________________
3. ____________________
4. ____________________
5. ____________________

Include rates of dividends and interest.

** see glossary*

Real Estate (Residence, Rentals, Vacation, Investments) — Use total value here; we will factor in mortgages later.

Include current values and purchase prices.

1. ____________________
2. ____________________
3. ____________________
4. ____________________
5. ____________________

Other Investments / Business Interests / Cars / Personal Property / Collectibles / Jewelry

1. ____________________
2. ____________________
3. ____________________
4. ____________________
5. ____________________

TOTAL ASSETS (Add all the values above): ____________________

LIABILITIES

Mortgages

1. First Mortgage Balance: ____________________
2. Home Equity Line: ____________________
3. Charge Accounts

	Company	Balance	Interest Rate	Minimum Payment
a.				
b.				
c.				
d.				

4. Lines of Credit

a. ____
b. ____
c. ____
d. ____

Include bank name, interest rates, number of months to pay off.

5. Car Loans

	Name	Vehicle	Balance	Monthly Payment	# Payments Remaining
a.					
b.					
c.					

6. Other Loans / Liabilities

	To Whom Owed	Terms	Interest Rate	Balance	Monthly Payment
a.					
b.					
c.					
d.					

TOTAL LIABILITIES (Add all balances above): ____________________

Now Calculate Your Net Worth

TOTAL ASSETS	-	TOTAL LIABILITIES	=	NET WORTH
____________	-	____________	=	____________

Evaluate Your Liabilities

Creditor	Balance Due	Monthly Payment	Interest Rate Ded./Non-ded.	Pay-Off Date # of payments remaining

Deductible interest includes your interest on your first mortgage and the interest on the first $100,000 of your home equity loan. Interest on the mortgage for a second home is deductible as well. In addition, interest incurred on loans to purchase investments is deductible.

Consumer interest in nondeductible. This includes credit card interest, car loans (personal) and other personal lines of credit.

Examine Your Home

FIRST MORTGAGE

Account Balance: ______________________________

Current Interest Rate: ___________________________

Number of Years Until Payoff: ______________________

HOME EQUITY LINE

Account Balance: ________________________

Current Interest Rate: ________________________

Fixed or Variable Interest Rate: ________________________

Maturity: ________________________

Purchase Price of Home: $______________ Current Value: $_______________

Improvements

	Description	Cost	Year
1.			
2.			
3.			
4.			

Purchase Price + Cost of Improvements = Basis of Home

Current Value - Basis = Capital Gain / Loss *(how much your value has grown or not)*

Capital Gains Issues to Note

Relatively new rules.

- If you are married and you file your tax returns jointly, *and* your capital gains is less than $500,000 *and* you have owned your home for at least two years, you do not have a taxable event when you sell.
- If you are single/widowed/or married filing separately, *and* your capital gains is less than $250,000 *and* you have owned your home for at least two years, you do not have a taxable event when you sell.
- If your capital gains exceed the above amounts (500/250) and you sell your home, you will have taxable capital gains to the extent the gains exceed the above amounts.

Prior to taking any action in this area, please remember to consult with a qualified tax advisor.

Home Equity Loans

Let's take a closer look at what home equity loans are and how they work.

According to current tax law you may borrow up to $100,000 of the equity in your home above the first mortgage amount from your original purchase and be able to deduct the interest in full on your tax return. You may use the proceeds for anything you choose.

> **For example,** you purchased a home for $150,000 and took a first mortgage of $100,000. The home goes up in value and now it is worth $300,000. Even though you have over 200,000 of equity in your home, you can only borrow up to an additional 100,000 if you want to deduct all the interest. **Now, to take this example a step further,** if you had refinanced your home along the way and took out equity from the home at closing, that amount is subtracted from the 100,000 that would be available from the home equity line. So, in the above example, had you refinanced the original mortgage a couple of years ago for 150,000 (thereby increasing the original loan amount by 50,000), you can then only borrow another 50,000 with your home equity loan and still deduct the interest.

Keep track of your borrowing

You can borrow an unlimited amount against your equity, credit providing, but the amount of interest you may deduct is limited to the amount attributable to the first 100,000 of debt incurred over the amount you mortgaged upon purchase. If you incur interest on a greater amount and can attribute the use of that money to the purchase of investments or home improvements, then you may be able to deduct the excess interest as investment interest expense. Check with your tax advisor.

Typically, one gets approved for a line and then has the ability to tap into the line at will. Payments on the line begin when you draw on it. Some lines require you to pay interest and a portion of the principal with every payment. With others, you pay interest only with a *balloon* after a period of years. That means that you pay only interest on the outstanding balance monthly and you will owe the entire principal at one time at a predetermined later date. As you pay down the balance of the loan, you continually free up funds for future use. *Be sure to consult with your financial advisor before entering into any agreements to see what is best given your personal circumstances.*

Don't waste your equity!

Having that open line can be a blessing or a curse. If you misuse this privilege, you must be aware that you are toying with the value in your home. So, be disciplined with your spending of these dollars. However, if you are making a large purchase that would require you to otherwise take a loan, then perhaps this type of financing would make sense. At least here the interest is probably deductible whereas consumer debt (i.e. car loan interest) is not.

In addition, if you are paying off multiple credit cards, then you might use this vehicle to consolidate them, lower your monthly payments and deduct the interest. Again, you are cautioned to consult with your financial/tax advisor before making any changes.

5 Your Checking Account

Balance Your Checkbook Once a Month Without Fail

One of the ways many people get into financial trouble is by not balancing their checkbooks regularly. If you do not balance your checkbook, you could have a math error or have missed a transaction that could cause you to bounce checks. In addition, the bank can also make an error. This can cause excess fees in your account and is a waste of your money. In addition, too many of these errors could ultimately hurt your credit rating.

Balancing Your Checkbook Is Really Very Easy!

It's really easy!

- First, figure out if all your deposits for the month were credited
- See how many checks that you wrote during the month cleared
- See if the bank agrees with your balance in your register.
- Subtract any bank charges and add in any interest earned.
- After adding the deposits that were not credited and subtracting the checks that have not cleared, your balance in your checkbook should match that on the statement.

If you are high tech and bank on line, you could have it even easier. All your transactions should appear daily, so you can balance daily.

Worksheet

Look at your statement. On the first page you will see a *Summary of Your Account.*

In your register, subtract any fees that are listed here, and add any interest earned to your checkbook balance, since they have been already accounted for. THEN, take the last figure on your statement, which is called *End of Month Balance* and put it on the first line of this worksheet.

End of Month Balance from statement: ____________________

Compare the deposits listed on the statement with the deposits in your register. List any deposits made that are *not on the bank statement*:

+ ____________________
+ ____________________
+ ____________________

Look at your check register.

(A) *Add the total of deposits made but not listed on the statement*: = ________________**(A)**

Check off, from the statement, the checks that have cleared. Check them off not only by check number but the amount actually subtracted. (Go back to the individual checks or copies to correct any discrepancies.) Put a check next to each cleared check. If a check has not cleared, use a yellow highlighter and mark it. Then list to the right any checks written since the last statement that haven't cleared. Go back to prior months and look for the yellow marks and see if those have cleared. If not, add them to the list at the right.

+ ____________________
+ ____________________
+ ____________________
+ ____________________
+ ____________________
+ ____________________
+ ____________________

(B) Add the total of the Outstanding Checks: = ________________**(B)**

Subtract the total of the Outstanding Checks from the ending balance and outstanding deposits (A - B). This number should equal your balance in your checkbook.

________________(A)

\- ________________(B)

= ____________________

If you have trouble, be sure to call your bank for assistance.

6 Reading Your Tax Return

Your Own Personal Best Seller

In this section, I will take you on a journey through your tax return by way of a series of questions you should have answers to. Take out your most recent prepared tax return and let's get started. If you do not have a copy you can obtain one from your tax-preparer or even the IRS. You should always keep a copy of your return for three years. If you pay someone to prepare them, they must give you a copy when your return is delivered. Jot down your answers as you go. Not everyone will have a tax return complex enough to be able to address all of these questions. As you find questions that do not apply, skip them and go on.

Tax Return Questions to Consider

1. What are your wages? Your spouse's wages? What will they be this year? (Any raises, promotions, etc.)

2. How much in taxable interest income do you receive? How much value do you have in investment vehicles that give you taxable interest? Do you reinvest or do you need the income for living expenses? Is the amount of money allocated to this area too great for your needs? Each person's answer to this will be different.

3. How much in taxable dividends do you receive? What are the sources? Do you reinvest or do you live on these dividends?

Don't skip any questions that apply to your return!

4. How many taxable capital gains did you have? How much control do you have over these amounts? What about capital gains distributions? Can you lessen the effects of these capital gains distributions?

5. Look at your capital gains from the sales of stocks and bonds. Could you have sold others at a loss to minimize your gains? In reporting the gains from the sales of investment real estate, did you reduce your basis by the amounts of accumulated depreciation? Check out your IRA – even though gains and losses there do not affect your taxes, they do affect your net worth.

6. If you have a Schedule C or a sole proprietorship business, have you taken a deduction for all the expenses you could have? What about office-in-home? Are you eligible? What about your health insurance premiums, have you deducted the most you can? Have you provided for a retirement plan? Is a sole proprietorship the best way for you to go? Have you opened a Keogh Plan, SEP or Simple IRA?

Are you keeping adequate records?

7. Do you have an IRA? Traditional or Roth? Which is better for you?

8. Did you rollover a pension? Where are those assets invested now?

9. What amount of tax are you paying on your Social Security benefits if you are receiving them?

Take advantage of all the deductions you are entitled to.

10. Look at your Itemized Deductions. Are you taking the most you can? Look at Charitable Donations. Are you deducting the mileage you use for your car when working on charitable activities? Are you adding up your Medical Expenses to rule out a deduction here or are you just making an assumption that you don't qualify?

Practice tax avoidance, not tax evasion.

11. What are you paying in tax? Are you a two-earner family? If so, is your family's tax liability equal to one of the incomes? If so, are you taking steps to reduce the burden?

12. Are you preparing your own return? If so, what sources of research are you using to keep current with the changes in the law? Are you sure you have taken the maximum deductions allowed by law?

If you prepare your own return, stay current.

13. Have you deducted for your childcare expenses?

14. If you paid estimated tax to your state, did you pay the last payment of the year before Dec. 31 to be able to deduct it on your tax return for the current year?

Now that you have learned even more about your financial situation and your tax liabilities, it will become easier to make some decisions relative to your investment strategies. You can more fully understand just where your tax liabilities come from. As we move forward in your financial planning, tax liabilities will become an issue when making investment decisions. You will need to examine the tax costs before selling assets and the tax ramifications of specific purchases. While investment decisions should not be made upon tax issues alone, taxes cannot be ignored. In the next section we will be discussing investment strategies that can serve to manage your tax liabilities in the future. The information you have gained in this section will be useful to you as we move forward in investment analysis.

A little knowledge goes a long way.

Remember that tax laws change regularly, and it is necessary to follow the changes. Strategies that are useful today could become obsolete tomorrow. If you prepare your own return it is even more vital that you stay current on the law. I still see returns where people are still deducting consumer interest on Schedule A: Itemized Deductions. That *has not been allowable* since 1986. One of the first ways to minimize your tax liabilities is to take the maximum allowable deductions on your return.

Tax planning is a process that extends all the way into the retirement years.

7 Retirement Planning

What is Retirement Planning?

It is the process of accumulating and managing investment assets during your working years and beyond in order to create and maintain an independent and comfortable standard of living for the rest of your life. Retirement planning also involves the setting up of safeguards to help protect against risk and a process for passing on your assets in a most efficient manner. Planning starts with setting goals for the short term as well as the long term. It is hard to plan when you don't know what you are trying to accomplish.

What Are Your Financial Goals?

Short Term (1 to 3 years)

1. ______________________________
2. ______________________________
3. ______________________________

Intermediate Term (3 to 10 years)

1. ______________________________
2. ______________________________
3. ______________________________

This is the time for some dreaming.

Long Term (10+ years)

1. ______________________________
2. ______________________________
3. ______________________________

For the remaining exercises and sections to make any sense, you need to get a handle on where you want to be. Without goals in mind, you are shifting aimlessly and you will not be able to adequately measure progress. With measurable goals, you will be able to monitor progress towards their achievement as you go and amend your route as necessary.

Your goals will change over the years and you will be able to accommodate for them as you go.

Part One Summary

Congratulations! You have taken the first steps toward achieving your goals. By now, if you have gone through the exercises, you should be feeling more organized and in control. You should have a better understanding of what you have and how to access it. If you make organization a priority, the systems you have set up should be maintained out of habit.

You are ready to take on the next two sections if you have mastered the exercises in this section. We will be using the information you have put together to build upon as we move forward. However, we will be using them in different ways and we will be looking for additional information as we move forward.

As time goes by and you accumulate more assets and accounts you will need to expand your process to include them. Perhaps you will expand to two or more binders or file spaces.

As you move on to the following sections be sure to reference the glossary at the end of this book to be sure you have mastered the language of money.

Checklist of organizational items you should have completed

1. A list of potential financial advisors.
2. Three ring binder with sections allocated to each investment/account
3. A file drawer with files for all your vital papers
4. Monthly budget sheet for at least a month
5. Proposed budget/actual amounts for the second month
6. An analysis of income/expenses
7. A Balance Sheet
8. Analysis of your debt/mortgages
9. The first worksheet for balancing your checking account filled out and "balanced"
10. An understanding of your tax liabilities
11. A list of your goals.

These are some of the materials you should have when going to see a financial advisor. Having a list of your assets and their values along with budget and liability information and a list of your goals makes the consultation with a professional more meaningful. The information you pull together in the next two sections will make you much more knowledgeable about your finances. Working with a professional will help you pull all the information together better.

Part Two

INVESTING FOR YOUR FUTURE

In **Part Two** you will learn to **Invest For Your Future**

This section will take you through the evaluation of your current assets, the concept of asset allocation, and then will demonstrate ways to help you track the performance of your assets in the future. You will learn how to read the financial sections of your newspaper to derive the maximum information. You will learn the meanings of various terms that will be useful to you as you move forward in your education process. We will explore various investment options and discuss the many forms of risk you face as you invest. The portfolio will be examined from the standpoint of the major asset categories and then we will look at the options within each class. The worksheets we have provided will assist you in the process of evaluating your investments. This will afford you the opportunity to learn and become more knowledgeable about your investments. For those of you just starting out, keep this information handy for the future as you grow.

For now, let's see just how many of the following questions you can answer easily. Don't be intimidated by them; just do it so that you will be able to measure your increased knowledge at the end of the section. When we are done, we will take out the questions again and try to answer them. Then we will compare our results. Hopefully, at the end, you will have made more sense of it all.

So, take out your Balance Sheet and get going. Jot down your answers and put them aside.

- What was the total return on your investments for last year?
- What is your year-to-date return?
- What is the percentage allocation of your assets in cash, stocks and bonds?
- What is the historical track record of the mutual funds you own?
- What is the rate of return in your IRA? 401k?
- How much have your assets grown since you purchased them?
- How much of the distributions from your assets are fully taxable?
- What is the return on your investments after taxes and inflation?
- What types of risk are you taking with your investments?

Your Goals and Your Investments 8

If you don't know where you are going, how will you know how to get there?

Let's take out your "goals" worksheet from Part One. In examining your goals, it is important to be realistic relative to the time frames. For example, a 30-year-old person might want to have a retirement goal of 45, but if they have not yet begun a savings program it might be unrealistic that such a goal can be accomplished under typical circumstances. Yet, if that person is about ready to receive a large inheritance or cash in on corporate stock options, that sort of goal could be appropriate in their situation.

Be realistic when setting goals!

This is why you need to have clearly defined goals as you enter the financial planning process. It puts your needs into perspective and helps you determine which investments are appropriate for you given these parameters. For example, if you have a cash need in the next year or two for a down payment on a car or a home, you would not want to invest that money into a 10 year illiquid investment. On the other hand, if you want to invest for the long term and you have at least a 10 year horizon, then keeping the money in a liquid money market may not be the correct choice given your set of circumstances.

It is important to look at your constraints. These might include family obligations, health constraints or any other set of circumstances over which you may not have control.

Be realistic; set goals that perhaps can challenge you but should be attainable. If you set unrealistic goals it will only serve to frustrate you and perhaps persuade you to make poor decisions relative to investment choices. You might invest more aggressively than you are usually comfortable with and ignore your risk tolerance levels.

When setting your goals, be realistic about the amounts of money you will need to satisfy your goals. Look at long-term asset and income needs and take inflation into account.

You have set down your goals in Part One of this course. Now review them and see if they make sense as you move forward with this plan. Amend them as necessary until you feel comfortable with them. Goals are not static. On the contrary, they are ever changing. You will need to amend and change course from time to time. What is

Life is ever changing.

appropriate now may not be appropriate next year. This is okay. This is all the more reason to track your investments and monitor their performance. When goals change, and you need to change directions with your assets you will need to have an understanding as to what assets are appropriate to change. You will need to have a solid handle on basis information to calculate tax consequences as well as how that repositioning might influence your asset allocation mix.

In this section we will discuss the various risks as they relate to your investments and other factors that may affect the outcome of your investment strategy. We will look at the economy and the business cycle as factors affecting your portfolio.

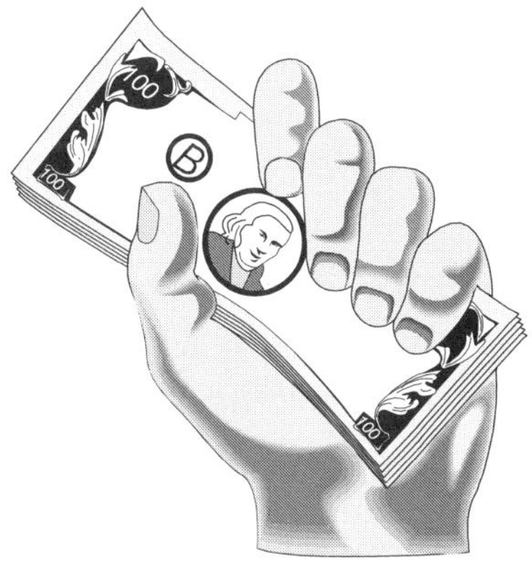

How To Plan Your Investment Strategy

9

Many factors go into the decision making process for investment evaluation and selection. Today, there are just so many choices and so many sources of information not the least of which is everything that we can find on the Internet. The problem is not in the availability of information but in the sorting and absorption of it. It is a daunting task to sort through the volumes of information and to determine just what applies in any one situation or set of circumstances. Determining what you should pay attention to and what to discard is difficult in a world where there are so many options. As you've probably noticed, as you read periodicals, newspapers or search the Internet, the ads each claim that their product is a great performer and is the best option for you. I have not seen an ad for an investment, yet, that claims to be mediocre in performance, or better yet, says that they may not be appropriate for your portfolio.

So, how do you decide?

The only way is to be forearmed with information about yourself, your goals and your risk tolerance level as well as a good solid understanding of investments. There are several concepts that you need to understand that will give you a firmer frame of reference. We will discuss the concepts of inflation, the economic picture, the business cycle, volatility, liquidity and marketability and risk management and how they can affect your money.

Be forearmed.

INFLATION

Even at low levels, inflation can affect your purchasing power. As prices rise, the dollars we have just don't go as far. This has the effect of actually shrinking our incomes. It can affect those who are on fixed incomes to a larger degree than many others. When

Protect your purchasing power.

we have a fixed amount coming in and prices go up, fewer goods and services can be purchased. Usually the fixed income comes from a fixed percentage of interest from your bonds, preferred stock, bank interest or a fixed pension. This is why it can be so important to keep some amount of growth-oriented investments in our portfolios even during the retirement years. As we work, we usually get raises and promotions. This helps us cope with the rising costs of living. However, during retirement, raises only come to those who make them come. This is by growing the portfolio and therefore living off a growing dollar amount of assets. As an example, if you set things up to live off a 6% income stream from your investments and the base continues to grow at say 8%, you allow for a potentially rising income dollar amount. However, if there is no growth and you depend on a fixed income from interest and dividends, there is no way to offset increasing living expenses.

You will always need growth.

In planning for a future income stream we need to first look at what it would cost to live in today's dollars. Then it is important to inflate those dollars into the future. It puts a perspective on what you will need to accumulate to accomplish your goals. Then you can decide just how much you need to put aside now to assure a standard of living in the future. When you do these calculations it could demonstrate a need to put a very high amount of money aside on a monthly basis now. Yet, when looking at your cash flow, those dollars may not be available for the savings level you might need. So what do you do? First of all, reexamine your goals. Perhaps they are too high. Secondly, reexamine your budget numbers to see if your day-to-day priorities are where they should be. Take out that budget analysis and re-examine it. Then come up with a dollar amount you could put away every month towards your goals. Thirdly, you may have to work a little longer or perhaps take on a second job to meet your goals.

Are your goals realistic?

THE ECONOMY

There are various issues that influence the investment world. Political pressures affect prices not only in the oil and gas industry but others as well. The indexes for consumer prices, employment, inventories and others directly affect the stock market and cause varying degrees of volatility.

Interest rate changes affect not only the market for stocks and bonds, but also the bottom line profits of corporations. As the cost of interest rises, the cost of doing business rises as well. Companies who borrow money to pay for inventory have a harder time getting financing and when they do, the cost is higher. Profits drop and other consequences follow. As far as our bonds are concerned, rising interest rates cause us to lose money in their net asset value. For example, if you own a bond earning 6% and interest rates in the open market are up to 8%, you would have to lower the price of your bond if you were to try to sell it. Why would anyone pay full price for a 6% bond when they could get 8% elsewhere?

Bond values fluctuate inversely with interest rates.

We need to be aware of the trends in the economy as it applies to the "New Economy". This is a relatively new phenomenon. The technology and biotechnology areas are new significant players in recent times. Yet they are volatile areas of the business community and old formulas for evaluation didn't seem to apply in years recently past.

BUSINESS CYCLE

The business cycle is and will always be with us. As the economy ebbs and flows, we find ourselves going from a recovery to an inflationary period into recession and yet another recovery. There is economic significance to each of these phases.

We have defined **inflation** and we have all experienced it to one degree or another. During inflationary periods, interest rates tend to peak out. Values of tangible assets such as real estate go up and peak. You tend to feel like the dollars you have just can't go far enough. Values of bonds are low and falling due to those rising interest rates. The stock market is usually shaky since the market does not like inflation. Money becomes tight and business usually contracts due to a capital shortage and shrinkage of cash flow since the products and services they purchase will also go up in price. Wage demands rise putting even more pressure on business. Prices rise in response. We begin to feel a little out of control.

The business cycle will always be with us.

What tends to follow is a **recession**. Just before this occurs it becomes a good time to buy fixed income investments and lessen the allocation to real assets. Interest rates begin to decline; fixed income investments rise in value and the demand for real assets declines. Unemployment usually rises during this period as businesses fight for cash flow. Sales are down and public sentiment is unsure and lacks confidence.

After a while, we start seeing the signs of **recovery.** The government begins to intervene by increasing money supply with the intention of stimulating the economy. The stock market will usually respond by rising in value and after some contraction, profits appear to begin rising again. It is a good time to sell fixed income investments during this phase since interest rates could potentially rise. It is a good time to be purchasing real assets since they will probably go up in value during the recovery and on the way to inflation yet again. The stock market usually improves during this phase as well. However, there are no guarantees.

VOLATILITY

This is what we experience as we watch stocks rise and fall in value at will and in response to the economic cycles and emotions of the public. Stocks are one of the most volatile of the liquid investments and tend to swing up and/or down on rumor, speculation, and emotion. The extent to how much of this you can live with measures your risk tolerance. Another factor influencing your tolerance of volatility is the time horizon of your goals. Most people can tolerate more volatility if their time horizon is a long one. For dollars we may need sooner, our tolerance may be lower. We have been witness to swings in market prices that occur in virtually hours and minutes. I have seen some stocks rise and fall by over 100 points within a few hours. Specific issues have varying degrees of volatility, commonly called "beta". It is a measurable value and you should investigate an investment's beta before you invest so that you will know what potential level of risk you are taking. You need to evaluate the investments you are looking at and decide which are within your risk and volatility tolerance level.

Understand your risk tolerance level.

RISK

Risk comes in various forms. Most people think of risk as the loss of their principal. However, we must first say that "all" investments have risk. This includes your savings account and money market. Let me explain.

Erosion of spendable dollars.

The first risk that I will discuss is **purchasing power risk**. This is the effect we all experience when we find that our money just doesn't go as far as it might have in past times. It is the erosion in our spendable dollars due to inflation. When we are on a fixed income we are more likely to experience the discomfort caused by this problem. We see the shrinkage in our spending abilities and the long-term effect is to decrease our standard of living. This type of risk comes with even the "safest" investments in savings accounts, CD's (Certificates of Deposit) and Money Markets. Following this section there is a worksheet to help you determine the long-term return from a typical CD.

** CD's are insured by the FDIC and offer a fixed rate of return, whereas the return and principal value of an investment in stocks fluctuates with changes in market conditions.*

Time horizon is an important factor in choosing investments.

Market risk is one that you might be intimate with. One needs to just turn on the news at night and listen to the financial report to hear about the rises and declines in the market. The greatest risk here is for the person who is invested for the short term or who might need to sell at short notice. You could be invested in a perfectly good stock or mutual fund and if you could ride out the markets, you might do well based on historical returns.* However, if you need to sell for an immediate need you could sell on an off day and take a loss. Market investments are not for short-term needs and goals. Nor should investments in this area be made with money that should be allocated to Cash or a Cash Equivalent. Everyone should have ready cash available for emergencies.

** Past Performance is no indication of future results.*

Political risk is out of the investor's control. Yet, performance is greatly affected by tax law changes, financial decisions made on political levels and political changes globally. Investments in companies abroad are not only affected by that region's economy, but by changes in leadership and politics there as well. Investments in companies in third world countries are affected by the political changes that occur there. We are living in a global economy and events impacting one country truly impact the others all around the world.

** Investing in emerging markets is especially volatile and involves unique risks such as currency fluctuations and political developments.*

Our investment choices are impacted by outside forces.

Our investments are impacted by **economic and business cycles**. We can be invested in a tremendous company or group of companies with promise of growth and income, but yet, as we move through the cycles of the economy, our investment will ebb and flow accordingly. Because money supply affects the way businesses operate, we will see gains and losses depending on the availability of cash and the ability to borrow. Inflation, recession and recovery have a great impact on the value of investments. Supply and demand can increase or decrease the need for specific products and services. This too affects the value of investments.

Interest rates, a subject of many discussions in the media, have a great impact on our investments. The higher the interest rates, the less profitable businesses become. It also becomes harder for businesses to find financing for their projects. The risk relative to interest rates also directly affects our investments in fixed income investments i.e. bonds, utility stocks and other income producing stocks. The value of those investments fall as interest rates rise and rise as interest rates fall. This inverse relationship can be a little hard to grasp at first.

Let's look at an example of how interest rates affect these investments. Just suppose you owned a bond yielding 5%. Interest rates rise and bonds with 6% yields are now available. You go to sell your 5% bond. Why would anyone pay you full price for a 5% yield when they can get a 6% yield? Therefore, you would have to discount the price for your bond to reflect its lower coupon and to be an equivalent value that would yield the market rate of 6%.

Think this through.

The opposite is also true. You own a bond yielding 7% and the interest rates drop so that the only bonds in the market were yielding 5%. You need to sell your 7% bond. You know you have something of value that the market is not offering. This would encourage you to increase the price you are charging for your bond.

For every 1% in interest change, there is usually an approximate 10% change in bond and fixed income values.

**The rates of return discussed here are hypothetical and do not represent the returns of any particular investment.*

What Is the Potential Effective Yield of a CD*?

Invest $10,000 at 3%**

(Use any interest rate you might be offered)

Income @ 3%	________________
Federal Tax @ 25%	________________
State Tax @ 8%	________________
Net after tax income [income - (Federal + State Tax)]	________________
Inflation @ a historical average of 4%	________________
Net purchasing power (Net after tax income - cost of inflation)	________________
Net rate of return after tax and inflation	________________

Net purchasing power/original investment)

* CDs and other Bank deposits aggregating $100,000 are FDIC insured and offer a fixed rate of return. Investments are not bank deposits and are NOT FDIC insured. Investment returns fluctuate and involve risk, including possible loss of principal. CDs are Certificates of Deposit issued by a bank.

** For illustration purposes only, does not represent any specific investment.

The Business Cycle

INFLATION

- Interest rates peak
- Prices rise
- Fixed investments at a low point

RECOVERY

- Interest rates rise
- Bond values fall
- Best to own tangibles
- Inflation heats up

RECESSION

- Interest rates fall
- Bond values rise
- Less economic output
- Rising unemployment
- Time to look at selling tangibles

10 Investments and Your Taxes

While it is never recommended that you make investment decisions based on tax ramifications alone, it is important to look at the tax consequences before you act. You will want to know how the yields on your investments affect your tax liabilities and whether using tax-free investments are in your best interest. It is also wise to look at using investment vehicles with tax deferral especially if you are in a high tax bracket.

In addition, once you are invested in a variety of investments, it is wise to calculate your tax liabilities prior to making a selling transaction. If you are invested in mutual funds, and switch among the funds in the family, each sale is a new transaction subject to taxation. And each subsequent purchase forms a new basis for the future.

Of course, this does not apply to those investments you may have in your IRA, variable or fixed annuities or other pension type plans. All transactions within those plans are not immediately taxable. This includes dividends, capital gains distributions, and other capital gains.

While taxes should not be the primary reason to buy or sell, you can't ignore them either!

Let us also distinguish between ordinary income, short-term capital gains and long-term capital gains. Ordinary income is taxed at the tax bracket you fall into based on all your adjusted gross income. Wages, business income and interest and some other investment distributions fall into this category. Dividend and capital gain are taxed at a rate lower than most tax rates. Passive income, income from activities where you do not have active participation i.e. real estate, leasing, etc is taxed at ordinary income tax rates that range from 10% to 35%. Some of these income items can be sheltered by passive losses in other businesses. Passive losses can only be used to shelter passive income. The one exception is individual rental real estate whose passive losses can be used against ordinary income up to a limit of $25,000 if your adjusted gross income is below $100,000 and this is phased out as your income rises between 100,001 and $150,000 of income.

Short-term capital gains are those from the sale of investments with a holding period of less than one year. Short-term capital gains are taxed at ordinary income rates. Short-term gains can be reduced by short-term losses or long-term losses. Excess capital losses over gains can be deducted up to $3000/year and the balance gets carried forward until it is used up.

Long-term capital gains are those that arise from the sale of assets held for more than one year. The maximum tax rate applied to this form of gains is 15% and 10% Federal depending on your income. So, even if you are in a 35% tax bracket for the rest of your income, your long-term capital gains are taxed at a maximum of 15%. If you have the option of waiting for the one year period to pass before you sell your investment it pays to wait. However, if you might lose more by extending the waiting period then don't put the tax issue up front.

There are complicated guidelines for this under current law!

You Can Control Your Tax Liabilities

There are tools and techniques that can be employed so that you can legitimately keep your tax liabilities to a minimum. These tools and techniques are completely sanctioned in the tax code and are perfectly legal. As a matter of fact, they are written into the tax code to make the applications of tax law fair. So for those of you who think that tax reduction planning is somewhat "wrong", it is not, as long as we are thinking **tax avoidance not tax evasion.** The following paragraphs will explain some of those techniques and tools.

Tax avoidance not tax evasion!

Tax Deferred Investing

In this category we have a group of investment vehicles that allow you to invest now, earn now, but pay taxes later. The contributions can be either pre-tax (i.e. Qualified pension plans) or after tax (i.e., most IRA's, annuities, life insurance cash values). The earnings are not taxed as earned but rather when they are received at some future date. (Roth IRA's are an exception)* Without loss to current taxation, compound interest has a greater impact on the investment's future growth. These types of investments typically have a 10% tax penalty plus income tax if you want to receive the proceeds before age 59½. Life insurance cash values offer you tax deferral but also ultimate liquidity since most of it is available at any time utilizing their loan features or in some cases pure withdrawals. You only incur tax on the amount of the withdrawals that exceed the total of all contributions.

**The information provided is from sources deemed to be reliable; however, it is not intended to substitute for competent legal or accounting advice. Please consult with a qualified attorney or tax advisor prior to implementing any of the strategies discussed.*

Tax Deductible

Beware of the new changes in tax law.

Anytime you can invest in a program that is tax deductible (i.e. pension plans), the tax savings you will see are equal to your combined Federal and State tax bracket. For example, if you are in a 25% Federal bracket and a 8% State bracket, you get tax savings of 33% of your contribution. A $10,000 contribution to a retirement plan will net you $3,300 in tax savings. It is always advisable to maximize the plans you may have available through your employer. The same holds true for all other deductions on your tax return. As you fill out Schedule A on your return and itemize your deductions you are benefiting in the same fashion. Even if you are not a homeowner and do not have interest and real estate taxes to deduct, do not assume you can't itemize. Since your state and personal property taxes are a deduction, combining that amount with otherwise nondeductible charitable expenses, investment interest and miscellaneous expenses could allow you to itemize. In addition, if you own a business, be sure to deduct all you are entitled to including office-in-home when appropriate.

Tax Write-Offs

Consult with your professional advisor.

When you invest directly in certain types of investments (i.e. real estate, equipment leasing and natural resources) you can deduct (write off) a portion of your investment expenses for depreciation as well as some operating expenses. *Depreciation is the cost of the investment deducted over its useful life.* It allows for you to have deductions beyond your out of pocket expenses. If you multiply the amount of the deduction (write-off) by your tax bracket, this will give you the tax savings available because of your investment into this program. This is another form of tax deferral as depreciation reduces the basis. Capital gains or ordinary income will increase upon the sale or other divestiture. These investments are illiquid and carry a high degree of risk and potential loss of principal is possible. These types of investments are not guaranteed or insured and are not for all investors. Absolutely do not get involved with such investments without reading the prospectuses or offering memorandums. Also, be sure to consult with your tax or financial advisor. Beware of people trying to "sell" these types of investments over the phone.

Tax Credits

Reduce your tax, dollar for dollar.

Tax credits are available by investing in certain industries such as low-income housing (otherwise also known as affordable housing). Tax credits are a dollar for dollar reduction of your tax liabilities, and may be available for more than one year from a single investment. Commitment of funds should only follow the advice of your tax advisor. It requires a long-term commitment and may or may not be appropriate in your situation. They are subject to special risks and individuals must meet specific suitability standards before investing. There is no guarantee of return of principal and it carries with it associated risks. However, it is one of the few investments where a onetime investment can offer many years of tax savings. Obtain a prospectus and read it carefully prior to investing.

Income and Your Investments

Take out your Balance Sheet from Part One, and let's examine your investments and how they affect your return. From this exercise you will determine just how much income you receive from each and whether that income is taxable or nontaxable. You will be able to see the return from your investments at least from the income side. Remember that even though you may reinvest the income and capital gains distributions, you still incur the tax liabilities. Also, in this exercise we are not looking at Total Return. Total Return is the income from the investment plus any gain or loss in value. We are only looking for the income side. The growth or loss of value can be addressed later on.

Investment Name	**$ Value**	**$ Dividend/Year**	**Dividends as a % of value (div/value=%)**	**Taxable/ Nontaxable**

The Scoop on IRA's

Everyone should open an Individual Retirement Account (IRA) as a means of saving for retirement. However, it is wise to understand the differences among them to see which is right for you. We have the Traditional Deductible IRA, the Traditional Non-Deductible IRA and the Roth. All three have a place for different people. However, the Roth IRA may have the best long-term value over the others for many people. All three have a $3,000 contribution limit or 100% of earnings whichever is less. (If you are over 50 years of age, you can contribute up to $3,500.)

Three types of IRA's.

If you are working for a company that does not have a pension program and neither does your spouse then you may be able to deduct your IRA contributions as you make them. However, if you and your spouse work for a company with pension benefits and even if only one of you have it available then there are limitations for the deduction of your contributions based on your income levels. Remember that because you are deducting the contributions and therefore contributing pre tax dollars, all the distributions are taxable upon withdrawal. You need to track your deductible and nondeductible contributions to assure that you do not pay tax twice on your nondeductible contributions. Both deductible and nondeductible contributions accumulate on a tax-deferred basis during your working years and both require that you take minimum distributions at age 70½. Both have a 10% penalty plus tax if you choose to withdraw prior to age 59½. If you die, both can be rolled over to your spouse's IRA on a tax deferred basis and then your spouse will need to begin withdrawing at age 70½ as well. Upon the spouse's death, the full amount (in the case of the deductible IRA) or the income portion (in the case of the nondeductible kind) is fully taxable to your other heirs.

The earnings are tax deferred!

A Roth IRA works quite differently. The contributions are not deductible and are limited to those whose incomes meet certain limitations. Earnings are not taxed. You can rollover a traditional IRA to a Roth providing your income does not exceed predetermined amounts. However, when you do the rollover, your entire traditional IRA becomes taxable in the year of the transfer. The plus here is that you have frozen the values subject to tax at today's values not those into the future. But, once in the Roth, if left undisturbed for 5 years it is never taxed again. For those with a Roth, there is no requirement to ever make a minimum distribution and your heirs will not owe income taxes upon your death. Between the tax deferrals and the compounding effects of investing, this is one of the most powerful ways to save for retirement, if you qualify.

Eligibility depends on your income!

** The information provided is from sources deemed to be reliable; however, it is not intended to substitute for competent legal or accounting advice. Please consult with a qualified attorney or tax advisor prior to implementing any of the strategies discussed.*

Asset Allocation 11

A properly balanced portfolio is one of the best ways to minimize risk. If you are spread over different asset classes then as swings occur in different categories, you only have parts of your assets subject to that swing. It is very rare that all areas of the economy would go down at the same time. Also, as we have learned from the discussion on risk, each category has its own set of risks. So therefore, we are spreading out our exposure to the various forms of risk.

Let's go back to Part One of this course and take out your Balance Sheet. Now, we are going to get more involved with each investment asset you own and try to get more familiar with its attributes and rates of return. We are going to be looking at your diversification* and asset allocation to see just how your money has been invested. We are looking to see whether your portfolio is balanced and whether the current allocation is appropriate for your goals.

Let's examine your balance sheet.

** Diversification cannot eliminate the risk of investment loss.*

With asset allocation we determine by percent just how much of our assets should be in each category. Once we make this determination, then we need to rebalance our portfolio as various segments grow out of proportion. We should take the excess growth in any one category and reallocate to other areas of opportunity. In that way, when the market swings in a new direction we will have captured the growth that we had.

Major Categories of Asset Allocation

Cash and Cash Equivalents

This category includes money in checking accounts, savings accounts, money markets, CD's, fixed annuities, and savings bonds. The funds are in cash or can be turned into ready cash without market risk or fluctuations in value. These assets are usually liquid and the principal is safe. What we have here is purchasing power risk since the interest on these assets is fixed and usually on the low side relative to other investments in other categories. Everyone needs some amount in this category and this varies with the size of the portfolio, age, goals, and risk tolerance.

Fixed Income / Mutual Funds

Here we have bonds, preferred stock and utility stock. We also have investments in mutual funds whose primary objective is to invest in these vehicles. It represents investments that derive most of their yield from dividends and/or interest. The bonds include corporates, U.S. Government, and Municipals. Preferred stock offers a fixed coupon as well. These are all interest rate sensitive as we discussed above. We do need to pay attention to total return here since the asset values fluctuate. So while we may enjoy what seems like a good rate of dividend or interest, if the value of the investment drops, then our total return can be a negative one. This, as well as any other investment other than cash, does not have a guaranteed return of principal. Allocations to this area should be determined with your advisor. The percentage allocated to municipal bonds should be weighed against your total tax liabilities. The lower your tax bracket, the lesser the value of holding such investments.

Growth, Stocks, Mutual Funds

Many ways to diversify here!

Here we are dealing with investments that typically are low dividend producers. Most of your total return comes from the potential growth in the investment. We can invest either domestically or globally in individual issues of stock or in mutual funds that have as their primary objective to invest in growth oriented stock. These can be in small companies, mid size or large cap. They can be in any industry. They can be blue chip or Nasdaq. Tax liabilities occur on the growth only when they are sold. Losses can be netted against gains. No matter where you are in the life cycle, you need to have some assets allocated to this category to try to keep up with inflation. There are market fluctuations in this category, some of which can be quite volatile. This is not meant for those dollars needed in the short run.

Real Estate

In an effort to diversify your portfolio into areas not affected by the market swings, an investor needs to look other places. You can invest in real estate in several different ways. First, there is the traditional way of owning a specific rental property, leasing it to a tenant and becoming a landlord. If that does not appeal to you, then perhaps you can invest with a group in a limited liability corporation or a limited partnership. These, just as in direct ownership of an individual piece of property, are not liquid and are not easily sold. They need to be listed for sale and then offers are made. This can take a while and should only be entered into with dollars that are not going to be needed for a 5- to 10-year or longer period. There are other ways to invest in real estate.

The most liquid way is in a publicly traded REIT (Real Estate Investment Trust). These operate in a similar fashion to a mutual fund in that various investors' money is pooled in a corporation designed to purchase property or invest in mortgages. The general manager directs the investment and management of the funds and passes on 95% of the income to the investor. The shares of this corporation are traded in the market and are available for liquidation as any other stock. REIT's offer you the advantage of owning real estate on a marketable basis and the disadvantage of having not only the risk of the real estate values fluctuating but that of the stock market as well. They have been known to fluctuate in value quite broadly.

Be sure to read prospectuses before investing in any security.

Operating Business

Again, in an effort to diversify your portfolio, investments in equipment leasing and other operating businesses are available to the small investor through limited liability corporations and limited partnerships.* It is only in the last two decades or so that the small investor has had the ability to get involved in such areas. Like investments of real estate, investments in these areas are for smaller percentages of your portfolio. You should expect little or no marketability for 5 to 10 years or so and should only be invested in if you can afford not to have access to the funds. In addition, as in any other investment, there are business risks associated with this and you could potentially have a loss of principal. The percentage of dollars allocated to this area as well as any area is a function of the size of your portfolio, goals, and risk tolerance. Be sure to read prospectuses before committing your funds to such an investment.

Consider all the possibilities.

** Direct Participation Programs (DPP's) may not be suitable for all investors. Redemption may be more or less than the original amount invested and there is potential illiquidity. Special risks are associated with a DPP's underlying investments and there is no assurance that the stated investment objectives will be met.*

Natural Resources

In this category you can invest directly in the oil and gas reserves* or through stocks and mutual funds. These stocks or mutual funds would have as their objective to invest in companies related to the industry as in oil and gas companies, companies that drill and companies that sell and develop the equipment that the other companies need. Of course, as in the real estate area, if you choose the stock and mutual fund vehicles, you have the market risk as well as the risk associated with the industry itself. This means business and political risk as well. Again, we put funds here as a diversification tool and also as a hedge against inflation.

** Direct Participation Programs (DPP's) may not be suitable for all investors. Redemption may be more or less than the original amount invested and there is potential illiquidity. Special risks are associated with a DPP's underlying investments and there is no assurance that the stated investment objectives will be met.*

Precious Metals

This is the most speculative of all the categories and is used as a token portion of some portfolios. We never put large amounts here and only in those portfolios that are large enough to stand the risk. Here, again, we can invest directly into the metals or in funds that own companies dealing in or mining these metals.

Asset Allocation Worksheet

Let's go back to your Balance Sheet, once again. Now that you understand the differences in the various categories of investing, I am going to ask you to place each of your investments into the following categories. Please use additional sheets if needed to complete this.

CASH AND CASH EQUIVALENTS

1. ______________________________
2. ______________________________
3. ______________________________
4. ______________________________
5. ______________________________

Total Cash/ Cash Equivalents ____________

CD's, money market, saving's accounts, checking accounts.

FIXED INCOME

1. ______________________________
2. ______________________________
3. ______________________________
4. ______________________________
5. ______________________________

Total Fixed Income ____________

Bonds, utilities, preferred stock.

GROWTH/STOCKS/MUTUAL FUNDS

1. ______________________________
2. ______________________________
3. ______________________________
4. ______________________________
5. ______________________________

Total Growth/Stocks/Mutual Funds ____________

Stocks and stock mutual funds.

REAL ESTATE

Only investments here — do not include your home.

1. ______________________
2. ______________________
3. ______________________
4. ______________________
5. ______________________

Total Real Estate ______________

OPERATING BUSINESS

Any business interest.

1. ______________________
2. ______________________
3. ______________________
4. ______________________
5. ______________________

Total Operating Business ______________

NATURAL RESOURCES

1. ______________________
2. ______________________
3. ______________________
4. ______________________
5. ______________________

Total Natural Resources ______________

PRECIOUS METALS

1. ______________________
2. ______________________
3. ______________________
4. ______________________
5. ______________________

Total Precious Metals ______________

Now take the total dollar amounts for each category and insert them in the following worksheet.

	Dollar Value	Percent of Total*
Cash and Cash Equivalents	______	______
Fixed Income	______	______
Growth/Stocks/Mut. Funds	______	______
Real Estate	______	______
Operating Business	______	______
Precious Metals	______	______
Total Invested Assets:	______	

** Dollar value per each category divided by the total = Percent of total*

CURRENT AND PROPOSED ALLOCATIONS IN PERCENT

	Current	Proposed
Cash/Cash Equivalents	______	______
Fixed Income	______	______
Growth/Stocks/Mut. Funds	______	______
Real Estate	______	______
Operating Business	______	______
Natural Resources	______	______
Precious Metals	______	______

The next part of this process is to analyze just what you have specifically within each category. You should investigate each individual investment you own.

Determine the Following

1. Divide the Fixed Income investments into Corporate Bonds, Preferred Stock, US Government Bonds and Notes, Municipal Bonds and Utility Stock (categorize mutual funds accordingly).
2. Divide your stocks and mutual funds into Blue Chip, Small Cap, Mid Cap, Technology, Health Care, Global, Communications, Energy, and any other sector you may own.
3. Within the Real Estate, Operating Business and Natural Resources categories, divide between liquid and illiquid investments.

Enter name of investment and dollar value under each category.

Fixed Income	Corp. Bond	Perf. Stk.	US Govt.	Muni's	Utilities	Other

Enter the name of the investment in first column and dollar value in the category column.

Stocks/Mutual Funds	Small Cap	Mid Cap	Blue Chip	Global	Tech	Health	Energy			

Real Estate	Individual Holding/ Illiquid	REIT/Liquid	Limited Partnership/ Illiquid

Now that you have broken down your invested assets into proper categories you will see just how much is allocated to each of the areas. You can make some determination as to whether the allocations are appropriate relative to your goals.

For example, if you are still working and retirement is way down the road, and you have most of your assets in cash and fixed income, you are probably not allocated properly. You, in all probability, should have a fair share in growth type investments to build for the future.

You need to diversify within each category.

As another example, if you are retired and have little in fixed income or cash you might be too aggressive and might need to reallocate to become more balanced.

As we pass through the different phases in the lifecycle your allocations may need to change. When we are younger we have the opportunity of time to allow assets to compound. Less needs to be set aside to achieve long-term growth because of the amount of the time ahead. In comparison an older person with the same goals will need to set aside more to achieve their goals because of the shorter time frame for growth. Again, a younger person can typically take on more risk since they have time to correct for mistakes and losses. After retirement there is less room for risk since the ability to recoup and reaccumulate after losses is greatly diminished.

Accumulation and Monitoring 12

Again, this is where working with a financial advisor becomes very effective. That person can be a good sounding board for you and your family. They can give you the advice you may need here to make the proper decisions for your future. Their experience actually working with these investments is useful when you are making choices for your portfolio.

Now let's examine your Mutual Funds and learn more about them. There are things you need to know in order to make proper decisions about not only those you have but those you might decide to purchase in the future. List all the mutual funds you own on the worksheet on the next page.

There is no substitute for experience.

Then determine whether they are commissioned products or 'no-load'. Typically, if you purchased them through your broker they have a commission, either a front end or contingent deferred sales charges. If they have a commission charge, determine just what that charge is, when it is/was paid and any ongoing fees. **"A"** shares have an upfront commission charge, **"B"** shares have a contingent deferred sales charge and **"C"** shares have an ongoing, usually 1% sales charge but no 12b-1 charge. See if you have the rights of accumulation to see if you can benefit from lower charges. Also, did you sign a letter of intent that would allow for lower charges if you buy more of the same fund within a year? Do your funds have a 12b-1 fee?

The best place to find this information is in the original prospectus, which you should have received, prior to investing and kept. If you do not have a prospectus on file for each of your funds, call the company and inquire about these facts. From now on, keep the prospectus for any future investments. Remember that if you purchase your funds from a planner or a broker, they must provide you with a prospectus before you buy. If you buy directly from the fund itself, they need to send you one before you fill out your application to purchase.

Other information that can be obtained from your prospectus includes how to purchase, how to sell, the mission of the fund, a description of the managers, past performance and other useful information. You should always read a prospectus carefully before you invest or send money.

Fund	Percent Load	a, b c shares	12b-1 fees	Rights of Accum.	Letter of Intent

What is a Mutual Fund Family?

A mutual fund family can consist of many individual funds with differing investment strategies and managers that market under one umbrella. This could include, among others:

Aggressive Growth Funds

Specialized Growth Funds

Equity Income Funds

Balanced Funds

International Stocks and/or Bonds*

Corporate Bond Funds

Government Securities Funds

Municipal Bond Funds

Typically, you can transfer from one fund to another within a family of funds at little or no cost. However, each move between the funds in a family is a TAXABLE EVENT, and the tax consequences need to be carefully monitored before each move!

* *International investments are subject to special risks, such as political unrest, economic instability, and currency fluctuations.*

How Much Cash Do You Really Need?

Add Up Your Cash Accounts

Checking ______________________

Savings ______________________

Money Market* ______________________

CD's ______________________

T-Bills ______________________

Total Cash Reserves: ______________________

What Are Your Monthly Living Expenses?

As a general guide you should have at least 6 months of living expenses in cash for emergencies. Take this number from your Budget Worksheet in Part One and multiply by 6

Monthly cash needs from budget x 6 = ______________________

Subtract your cash needs from the total cash reserves available. If there is a surplus, then you may begin to invest. If there is a deficit, you need to work on accumulation and adjusting your cash outlays. Go back to the budget section.

* *Money Market funds are neither insured nor guaranteed by the U.S. Government.*

Dollar Cost Averaging

An Efficient Method of Accumulating Assets

Strategy A: Lump Sum Investment, No Dollar Cost Averaging

Invest $500 Share Price: $10/share = 50 Shares

Strategy B: Dollar Cost Averaging

Invest $100/month for 5 months

Month 1:	$100	$10/ Share	10 Shares
Month 2:	$100	$5/Share	20 Shares
Month 3:	$100	$20/Share	5 Shares
Month 4:	$100	$1/ Share	100 Shares
Month 5:	$100	$8/Share	12.5 Shares
			147.5

Total invested: $500

Total Shares Purchased: 147.50

Average Cost per share: $3.39

These numbers are for illustration only. It is unlikely that you will find an actual mutual fund that will fluctuate in value according to this pattern. While this strategy is frequently used, it is by no means a guarantee of success. Regular investing does not assure a profit or protect against a loss in declining markets. Dollar cost averaging involves continuous investments in securities, regardless of fluctuating price levels. Investors should consider their financial ability to continue purchases through periods of low price levels. Use this with other accumulation strategies.

Please study the prospectus for any mutual fund you may choose in order to make a proper decision.

Systematic Withdrawals

Just as you use systematic savings in the Dollar Cost Averaging program you can do the reverse with your mutual funds. If you systematically take out an amount less than the average performance of the fund you will have an income stream coming from the fund and still have the potential for growth. There is a risk here however. If the fund under-performs, you will be eating into your principal. In order for this strategy to work, the fund needs to perform at a rate greater than that at which you are making your withdrawals. To do this, look for a fund with a strong long-term track record and then MONITOR, MONITOR, MONITOR. If you find the value is being eroded stop and reevaluate to see if this is still the way for you to go. Past performance is in no way to guarantee or promise future results.

Monitoring Your Progress

Once you have organized and positioned your portfolio in appropriate vehicles, your most important job begins. You cannot put your portfolio into autopilot and expect it to manage itself. Portfolios, like a garden, need tending both often and consistently. Monitoring each investment, as well as the overall allocations, is essential in order to help you reach your goals.

Monitor your assets.

You will probably pick good investments at the time you make your choices but things change that can affect their future performance. This can include changes in fund managers, the philosophy of the fund, its mission or just changes in the economy that affect the results. It is the savvy investor that monitors these types of changes and makes the necessary decisions along the way.

In addition, if you were fortunate to have a good return in any one category of the allocation, it would be wise to take some profits (after you review the tax costs) and move those profits to a category that might not be doing as well right now but has signs of promise for the future. Maintaining the percentage allocation is important to keep in touch with your goals. Sometimes goals change. Then it is advisable to revisit the allocation percentages and readjust them accordingly.

On page 80 is a sample of a spreadsheet that you can reproduce to assist you in the monitoring of your portfolio. Let's look at the spreadsheet. In filling it in we are looking for some specific information. This process needs to be done consistently and at least quarterly. We want to track the performance of the individual investments in each category of allocation and then we want to track the performance of each category itself. We want to note if a specific investment is lagging in the performance and then research why. We want to see if any specific sector is lagging and then how our individual investments are performing vs. their peers. We want to see if the percentage allocation to each category is remaining constant or is one out performing the others. Is one totally under performing? Is this change in performance short term or has it been going on for two or more quarters? What is going on in the economy that might be affecting performance? Are all the fund managers in place or has there been a shift in fund management?

A continual source of information is necessary for good decision-making.

We recommend this be done quarterly so that you are keeping up with changes and remaining in a high state of awareness about your money. In my practice this is a typical approach.

PERIODIC ASSET ALLOCATION REVIEW SYSTEM Page 1 of 1

NAME
SS #
DATE

CODES

1- JT	6-Sep IRA
2-Individual	7a-Keogh/MPP
3-Individual	7b-Pension/PSP
4a-IRA (H)	8-Trust
4b-IRA (W)	9-529 Plan
5a-ROTH IRA (H)	
5b-Roth IRA (W)	

ASSET CLASS/ FUND FAMILY	INVESTMENT	ACCOUNT #	CODE	VALUE DATE	VALUE DATE	BUY/SELL TRANSFER	UNREALIZED GAIN/LOSS $	%
CASH & CASH EQUIV.								
	Cash							
	Sub-total							
FIXED INCOME								
	Sub-total							
STOCKS/MUTUAL FUNDS								
	*****International*****							
	Sub-total							
	*****Domestic*****							
	Sub-total							
	Total Stocks/Mutual Funds							
OPERATING BUSINESS/REAL ESTATE								
	Sub-total							
NATURAL RESOURCES								
	Sub-total							
	GRAND TOTALS							

13 Reading the Financials

Reading the financial pages of your newspaper should provide you with ongoing information about your tradeable investments. In the business section (especially on Sunday) you will usually find information on Mutual Funds listed by fund families with their funds listed individually. You will find purchase prices and sale prices along with year-to-date performance information.

Understand what you read.

You can also find some bonds listed. In addition, you will find the stock pages listed alphabetically by exchange (i.e. Nasdaq, NYSE). There are usually many columns to decipher if you are to derive the maximum information. On the next page we will detail the columns and make it easier for you to read.

People avoid reading the financials because either they are not interested or they don't understand. You can't afford not to be interested; it's your future financial security that is at stake. Now you will understand because of all your efforts here. There is no excuse. You should feel fully empowered to take this on.

Hi/Low in Past 52 Weeks	Stock Symbol	Dividend/ Share	Yield	P/E Ratio	Number of Shares Traded that Day '000s	Hi/Low that Day	Price Last Trade that Day	Change in Today's vs. Yesterday's Close
30 1/8, 36	ABCD	.16	.6	25	312111	30, 37	35	+2
1	**2**	**3**	**4**	**5**	**6**	**7**	**8**	**9**

How to read the financials

1. The high and low price of that stock in the past 52 weeks. It is usually better to buy the shares nearer to its low than its high.
2. The Corporation stock symbol.
3. The annual dividend per share (last dividend on an annualized basis)
4. Current yield of the stock based on the annual dividend (3) divided by the current share price (8).
5. Price/Earnings multiple (P/E Ratio) of the stock, which is determined by dividing the closing price (8) by the latest 12 months earnings per share (EPS). The lower the P/E Ratio of the stock you purchase the better the value of what you purchase.
6. The number of shares that were traded that day shown as sales in '000s. A sudden surge in the number (#) of shares traded could be a warning sign for the better or worse. You should investigate that if you are following a stock.
7. The highest and lowest price that the shares of the company traded for on this day. The greater the spread, the more volatile the stock.
8. The price at which the stock last traded for the day.
9. The amount of change from this day's closing price (8) as compared to the closing price the day before. Again, the wider the swings from day to day the more volatile the stock is.

Part Two Summary

At this point you should feel real proud of yourself. You have organized your paperwork and your documents. You have your checkbook balanced. You have your budget under control and you have a current Balance Sheet.

Keep up the good work!

In addition, you now understand your Asset Allocation and have made a thorough analysis of your existing portfolio. For those of you just starting out, you know what you need to do as you begin to invest and save. You have become more astute relative to understanding what you are reading in the financials and that will serve to help you learn even more. You should feel empowered now to make those changes and start to move forward. You should also feel confident that you know the basics and that you are no longer intimidated by information.

Let's see how you really did. Let's repeat the little quiz you took at the beginning of the chapter.

How are you doing?

- What was your total return on your investments for last year?
- What is your year to date return?
- What is the percentage allocation of your assets in cash, stocks, and bonds?
- What is the historical track record of the mutual funds you own?
- What is the rate of return in your IRA? 401k?
- How much have your assets grown since you purchased them?
- How much of the distributions from my assets are fully taxable?
- What is the return on my investments after taxes and inflation?
- What types of risk am I taking with my investments?

How do your answers compare? Are they different? Were you able to answer all of them this time around? Hopefully you have a better handle on the answers or at least know better how to find them.

As you move forward to the next chapter, you will revisit some of this information and yet will be using it in a different way. We will be talking about your estate assets and risk management. Risk management will be dealt with from a different perspective than the one in this section.

Part Three

Protecting Your Estate

In **Part Three** you will learn to **Protect Your Estate**

Whew! You have been working very hard to organize and learn what it takes to develop a financial plan for you and your family's future. Hopefully, you have successfully completed the exercises in the past two sections. If not, be sure to follow up before you begin this section. You will need the information derived from the exercises in the last two sections to be able to fully benefit from this section.

In this section, we will be discussing issues relative to the protection of your assets both now and in the future. Risk management issues in this section will deal with unexpected disabilities and premature death. We will work with risk management concepts to assure that your goals are met even if you meet with the unexpected. Life insurance needs will be examined and we will explore the various types of coverage and when they are appropriate. There is a section on planning for incapacity that is of value whether you are 25 or 75. As a matter of fact, some of this information will prove useful for those in the "sandwich generation" and are caring for elderly parents or other relatives. We will look at the proper ways to title assets and the need for the coordination of those titles with your wills and trusts. We will be examining the best ways to preserve your estate from shrinkage due to estate and inheritance taxes as well as gifting techniques, both personal and charitable.

Keep the other two sections handy as you work through this part. We will need your budget worksheets, cash flow worksheets, balance sheet, asset allocation, and your insurance policies and retirement plans.

What Is Estate Planning? 14

It is the accumulation and preservation of your assets during your lifetime and the distribution of your assets both during your lifetime and upon your death in a meaningful, cost effective manner.

We have discussed prudent methods of accumulating assets as well as methods to assist in the preservation and management of those assets during your lifetime. It is in this section that we will deal with the protection and disposition of your assets so that your heirs will be taken care of properly. We will be discussing various forms of insurance that should be considered. In addition, we will be discussing techniques relative to reducing your estate tax liabilities as well as probate expenses to ensure that more of what you have accumulated gets distributed to your heirs in accordance with *your* wishes. In addition, we will explore some gifting techniques as well as the proper titling of your assets.

Conserving your assets and passing them on.

Proper estate planning is part financial planning and part legal. You will learn about concepts in this section. This will prompt you to think about how you want to distribute your estate and who should be in charge of doing so. It might also prompt intergenerational family discussions. All of this is as it should be.

However, to implement wills and/or trusts, you must speak to an attorney. Financial planners do not draft documents nor do they provide legal assistance. Rarely, you will find a financial planner who is also an attorney – we recommend working with an attorney who specializes in estate planning. That person should be up to date with the latest tax and estate law changes, as well as the best techniques to accomplish your goals.

Again, there are many software packages and programs on the Internet for do-it-yourselfers. We DO NOT RECOMMEND any of them. There is no good substitute for an attorney. Just having a document is not enough. They need to stand up with integrity when they are needed. Also, please review your estate plans regularly (at least every three years), especially if someone is born, someone dies, someone gets married or divorced or you move to a new state.

Well, let's get going on this final section!

15 Risk Management

You have set goals both for the short term and the long term. You have hopes and dreams for your families and want to see them realized. During the child rearing years most people hope to never have to uproot their children due to a sudden death of a parent or to prohibit their ability to get an education because of a lack of funds. We want our spouses to enjoy a standard of living that they have become accustomed to and we want to be able to retire in the comfort we dream about.

Yet, all of this could be taken away from us due to a sudden death, an illness, or an accident. As you plan for growth you must plan for these contingencies. Once an event occurs it is too late! We will take you through a process to examine your insurance program in the following pages so you can begin to determine:

- If you have the proper amount of insurance?
- If you have the proper kind of insurance?
- If all your risks are covered?

The Risk of Loss of Income and Assets During Your Working Years and Beyond

During your working years, you have obligations on a regular basis to cover bills and to prepare for other expenses. If you are working your budget correctly, you are also saving money regularly and investing to accumulate funds for your short and long-term goals. Most of what you bring home each week is accounted for and there is very little of what comes home that you can do without.

However, that paycheck can stop. Of course, you can get fired. But then you can find a new job and move on. But what if you have an accident or develop an ailment that prevents you from working for several months or from ever working again. This can happen at any age to anyone and for no apparent reason. As you age, illness becomes the primary reason for loss of income. During your working years there is a greater probability of illness than death. If you cannot work and bring in money, then the money you have needs to be spent to cover the cost of your care beyond what health insurance will cover. So the dollars you have saved for retirement and college education for your kids could easily be spent away. This outlay is in addition to the day-to-day expenses that won't go away just because you can't work.

We can follow this into retirement. "Old fashioned" pensions are becoming a thing of the past where you retired and received a decent income for life. We are all becoming much more reliant on our own devices for retirement in the way of investing our assets in 401k plans, IRA's, and personal investment plans. Social Security payments and the income from these sources is how most people put together their retirement income stream. What most people forget is that if they become ill during retirement or even before, and become totally incapacitated, their health insurance and Medicare will not cover their costs of care beyond 100 days. At that point, they are on their own for the cost of care. At-home nursing can run upwards of $20/ per hour and care in a facility can run over $150/per day. For a month we are looking at $5000-7,500 of outlay straight out-of-pocket. One does not have to be a mathematical genius to see how this can wipe out most family's estates in a short period of time. It is these assets that the family is dependent upon for an income stream that gets wiped away. Then what? If there are no assets, there is no income.

Prepare for the worst and hope for the best. At least you will be covered!

Medicaid will not kick in until you have spent down most of your assets and left yourself and your family impoverished. For a single person, that amount is under $5,000 in most states and for a married couple it is in the $80,000 range according to recent information from Medicaid. Your well spouse is entitled to only approximately $1,800 month in income above your cost of care.

So, as you can see, you can be wiped out easily as you watch your hopes and dreams for yourself and your family drown with your incapacity.

There are ways to protect yourself, your family and your assets. During your working years you need to be protected by **Long Term Disability** insurance. This type of coverage will help you replace some of your lost income stream. It will not replace 100% but it will replace 60% or so on a tax-free basis. So while this does not cover the cost of care, it covers some of the everyday bills we all have. The cost of care will still come from your assets. For many, this disability coverage exists with the company you work for as a benefit. While it is optional from the benefit standpoint it truly is not optional for your financial well being. No matter what the cost, it is worth it. *If you feel you can't afford the premium, just think what it might be like to cover your total expenses without any income.* Better be a little tight now than totally broke later. Remember you cannot assume the coverage you have is adequate, however. Review your employee benefit book or talk to a financial advisor.

You need to be sure to check these two provisions

1. **What is the definition of disability?** With this type of coverage it is vital to understand the criteria for making a claim. Unlike life insurance, whose criteria is simple, this type of coverage can have many restrictions. The most liberal is the definition of disability that will cover you if you cannot perform the duties of your own occupation. At least, here, you can work at a less qualified position and supplement your payments. If your policy says you cannot work in any occupation, then you are restricted and not well covered.

2. **What are the benefits to which you are entitled?** Of great importance is when you can begin collecting and for how long. If you are still working then it is important to have lifetime coverage. Social Security disability is hard to qualify for and is limited to those disabilities expected to end in death. Usually, we recommend a waiting period of 60 days before benefits begin if there are enough personal resources to last for that period. The shorter the waiting period, the higher the premium. We usually recommend lifetime coverage since we can't predict when an illness may heal so that you can resume employment. In addition, you should check to see that a high enough percent of your income is being replaced with the coverage you have. Even though you are covered to some degree at work, you can supplement it with private insurance if you can qualify. This applies to those who are government employees as well. Remember, you can only purchase this when you are well.

If you are over age 45 (some companies will issue it earlier) you are eligible to purchase **Long Term Care** insurance. This coverage will cover the cost of those extra expenses for home health care and nursing home expenses. This will have the effect of protecting your assets from the ravaging costs of this type of care. Instead of writing checks out of your assets, the insurance company covers them to the extent of your purchase. However, since the terms of collecting this type of coverage is vague as in Long Term Disability you need to be aware of the terminology involved as well as common provisions you should look for.

Terms that need to be defined

There are several terms that need to be defined so that the language you will see on the proposals makes sense.

1. **Waiting Period** – This is the time you will have to wait before receiving benefits. Some policies can be purchased with a 0-day wait, 20 days, 60 days, 90 days and up to one year. This is individual and based upon your ability to cover costs for a short term. Also the longer you wait to receive benefits the less you will spend on premium. If you are eligible for Medicare, the first 20 days will be covered in full; the next 80 have a $100 deductible, which can then be covered with Medi-gap insurance. After the first 100 days, you are on your own.
2. **Benefit Period** – This is the length of time you will actually collect benefits. You choose this up front when you purchase the policy. This can vary from 2 years to lifetime.
3. **COLA (Cost of Living Adjustment)** – When you purchase a daily benefit amount you need to provide for a cost of living adjustment in order to cover the increasing costs over the years due to inflation. You can have a simple benefit or a compounded benefit.
4. **Activities of Daily Living** – These are the routine activities of daily living such as dressing, eating, toileting, ambulating, grooming. Your ability to collect the benefits purchased is based on your lack of ability to perform these functions.

Features to look for

You will want to look for the following features and be sure you are getting them in your policy:

1. No prior hospital stay requirement before you can receive benefits
2. Coverage for custodial, intermediate and skilled care
3. Coverage for Alzheimer's disease
4. Coverage during occasional hospital stays in order to reserve your bed for return.
5. Coverage for assistance at home for housekeeping, cleaning and unskilled care
6. Respite care for caretakers
7. Waiver of Premium during periods of confinement
8. Training of Caregivers
9. A well rated insurance company that has an excellent claims payment history (either the company or the advisor selling you the product should provide this information)

The newest wrinkle in buying long-term care is the tax treatment of premiums and benefits. Now, starting in 1997, the premiums for long term care are deductible (graduated amounts depending on age, the maximum is $2,500 for each spouse over the age of 70) as a medical expense subject to a floor of 7.5% of your adjusted gross income. The benefits remain tax-free unless they exceed $175/day. Nursing home expenses are deductible as medical expenses as well.

Ask about a spousal discount if both you and your spouse are applying. Check with your associations and organizations to see if they have a group plan you can apply to.

Loss of Life

Life insurance is a very different subject. It is quite obvious how you collect on this type of insurance. You die; your family collects. There are justifiable reasons for purchasing this type of insurance. When one of the breadwinners dies, it leaves not only an emotional void in the family but a financial one as well.

Plans and dreams may be on the line and if there are not enough assets to invest for income, some major changes need to occur. Usually the surviving spouse either needs to go back to work full time in a career that pays well or takes on a second job. This, of course, puts a strain on the family. Just at the time when one parent dies, the other is taken away for increased employment obligations. Certainly, this is not desirable but becomes necessary. The goals of providing for a college education and other lifecycle events are highly jeopardized.

If, however, enough assets are available to invest for income, then the surviving spouse has options. Perhaps part-time employment will suffice for a while, perhaps remaining with the full-time position is viable but there will be no need for a second job. Knowing that the kids can go on to college, the family home need not be sold, and weddings and other lifecycle events can happen relieves so much pressure. The family's hopes and dreams can still stay intact.

For most families, however, the accumulation of sufficient assets is not yet complete. For many, it has not really even been started to any serious degree. What are they to do? It is for those folks that life insurance really makes sense. There is no other way to create an estate immediately in the event of a catastrophe. Life insurance is the only way to raise sufficient assets for investment when there are little or none after someone dies. How else can you purchase a lump sum of money for pennies on the dollar?

We will move on to discuss the various types of insurance and where they make sense. Then we will provide you with a worksheet that will help you determine just how much life insurance you should be considering. Again, remember that while there is a cost for the insurance and it will come from your budget, you can't afford to be without it. Without it you could be left with no budget at all.

Types of Insurance

There are three basic types of insurance: Term, Whole Life and Universal life. Within these categories there are various alternatives. We will take these one at a time and hopefully it will help you understand the product better. This way, when you sit with your advisor, you will better understand what you are purchasing. Many people become so overwhelmed as they discuss it that they just give up and never purchase it. Many people turn away because they don't see the value. Yet, none of them would own their home without fire insurance or liability insurance for fear that they would "lose" everything if the house burned down. **Some people don't seem to value their ability to produce income as highly as the loss of their homes. Why is that?**

Term Insurance

This provides a pure death benefit. As long as the premiums are paid on time, the company will pay the death benefit to your heirs when you die. If you stop paying the premium, the policy will lapse and you will no longer have the insurance. There is no equity build up and no cash value. The premiums, while low at early ages, goes up with age and becomes quite expensive when you are ready to retire. It is usually used to purchase larger amounts of insurance at younger ages where cash flow might be limited or to supplement some amount of permanent coverage. Now you can buy term insurance to fit various time periods of need. For example, you can purchase 1 year renewable, 5 year, 10, 15, 20, and I have seen 25 and 30 year as well. The premium for one-year term (annual renewable) goes up with age each year. It automatically renews if you continue to pay the rising premium. The others have level premiums for the period you purchase for the time indicated. Term insurance with a fixed premium for a period of years is easier to budget for and your total outlay is defined up front. Death benefits remain level. There is another type of term insurance that has been called "mortgage insurance". This type maintains a level premium but the death benefit drops with time. This becomes very expensive in the long run. In general, people do not keep term insurance into retirement since the premiums are prohibitive at later ages. In addition, at later ages, the need to provide assets to generate income may not be as great.

Whole Life

Whole life was developed to provide an alternative to term insurance and allow people an option for permanent insurance. It allows for the cash buildup or equity. It costs more than term at early ages but premiums stay level and may even end at retirement leaving you with a paid up policy. The cash accumulates on a tax-deferred basis but unlike retirement plans and annuities, the cash value is available for loans at favorable rates with no tax consequences. The interest is tax deferred and is only taxable when you surrender the policy. This type of insurance is available on a fixed interest and variable basis. The fixed interest is determined by the insurance company and is compounded. The variable policy has a separate account for the accumulations and investment opportunities are available from stocks, to bonds and money markets. Since there is less predictability in the investment structure, death benefits can vary with values. Since this is a permanent form of insurance, it allows people to retain coverage into retirement at no cost in many instances. The advantages of this type of coverage include the built in guarantees for the death benefit. However, this type of insurance offers little flexibility as compared to universal life.

Universal Life

This is a newer type of insurance, only around since the late 70's, early 80's. It is a product that combines similar features of whole life and term but offering a great deal more flexibility. It is also a permanent life product that allows you to build equity at a current rate of return. Basically, you make deposits into a cash pot that accumulates at a market rate of interest on a tax-deferred basis. Each month, money is taken to cover the cost of the death benefit (a term like coverage within the policy). The balance grows. Your outlay stays fixed and if the cost of the death benefit rises to a point that your contributions don't fully cover it, the cash value decreases to cover those additional charges. This is a matter that needs tracking. As the cost of the term insurance death benefit grows, you will be using up more and more of your cash account and if not watched you could accidentally lapse the entire policy. This can be avoided by depositing additional cash into the policy.

Which type is right for you?

Again, the cash value can be invested in a fixed account with interest that varies with the market. Or, the "separate accounts" can be invested in a portfolio of stocks, bonds and money markets that you can exchange among. The cash value is available to the owner of the policy either through loans at favorable rates or by simple withdrawals. Again, only the amounts that exceed the total of the deposits are taxable. You can structure your payments to stop at retirement or sooner based on specific guidelines. Usually the cost is less than for whole life and the flexibility is much greater. Yet, the coverage is permanent as long as there is enough money in the pot to cover the cost of the death benefit.

How Much Life Insurance Do You Really Need?

You need to explore both your lump sum cash needs and your income needs. To begin you need to gather some information about you and your family.

Let's go back to the worksheet where you listed your short term, intermediate term and long-term goals. Evaluate your priorities here and determine which of those are of highest priority and which are an absolute must. For those that are an absolute must, put a dollar amount to those priorities for your family. Divide them into those that represent lump sum needs i.e. college funding, weddings, etc., and those that are income stream oriented, i.e. comfortable retirement lifestyle. We will come back to this later.

Plan for your needs.

Now, go to your budget worksheet. Take a hard look at your spending habits and determine which expenditures are absolutely essential to maintain the family. Then determine what those expenditures might be without either you or your spouse in the picture. Look at what might decrease and what expenditures might increase because of the changed situation. Then look at the dollars coming in to the family. Determine first what you bring in currently and what can that be reduced to if either you or your spouse was to die prematurely. Think through priorities and the issues of work, child raising and other responsibilities to determine what you or your spouse might do in the event of a premature death. I know this is not a pleasant conversation to have and the tendency is to deny the possibility. However, pre-planning is essential and you need to be realistic with your approach to this issue. Come up with an annual income figure that would be absolutely necessary to keep the family going. We will use that figure later.

Let's take a brief look at Social Security benefits. If you are eligible for benefits because you have been contributing to the system you need to understand the limitations for surviving spouse benefits and children benefits. If you are a surviving spouse, with no children under the age of 16 and you are under the age of 62, there are no benefits. If you are a surviving spouse with children under the age of 16 you are entitled to benefits until your youngest child turns age 16. At that point, benefits stop until the spouse turns age 62. The amount of potential benefits is available to you by writing to the Social Security office to get an estimate of benefits. Your children are eligible to receive benefits until they are age 18. After that they are no longer eligible even if they are full time students. All of this will be taken into account as we move through the worksheet on the next page.

Any pension benefits you may have, either 401k or IRA would probably be rolled over to an IRA for your spouse and not touchable in that case until your spouse turns 59½. If your spouse were to take the funds sooner than that age, not only will there be income tax on the amount withdrawn but an additional 10% penalty as well.

What your spouse needs if you die first

If you die first, the following needs will apply to your spouse:

1. Lump sum needs:

a. College funding ______________

b. Wedding ______________

c. Payment of a debt ______________

d. Other (i.e. final expenses) ______________

Total Lump Sum Needs: ______________

2. Potential Sources of Income:

a. Spouse's salary ______________

b. Your Survivor pension ______________

c. Social Security ______________

(just until youngest child is 16)

d. Investment Income ______________

e. Other ______________

Total Potential Sources of Income: ______________

3. **Ongoing Expenses from Cash Flow Analysis** ______________

4. **Annual Shortfall (3-2)** ______________

5. **Capital Needed for Investment to Cover Income Shortage** ______________
(#4 divided by __%, or the percentage income you can expect to get by investing a lump sum of capital to get a reasonable amount of income. At this point, we use a 6% discount rate.)

6. **Amount of life insurance you would need (1+5)** ______________

7. **Amount of life insurance you now own + liquid investible assets** ______________

8. **Amount of life insurance you need to purchase** ______________
(6 – 7)

What you need if your spouse dies first

If your spouse dies first, the following needs will apply to you:

1. Lump sum needs:

a. College funding ______________

b. Wedding ______________

c. Payment of a debt ______________

d. Other (i.e. final expenses) ______________

Total Lump Sum Needs: ______________

2. Potential Sources of Income:

a. Spouse's salary ______________

b. Your Survivor pension ______________

c. Social Security ______________

(just until youngest child is 16)

d. Investment Income ______________

e. Other ______________

Total Potential Sources of Income: ______________

3. **Ongoing expenses from Cash Flow Analysis** ______________
4. **Annual Shortfall (3-2)** ______________
5. **Capital Needed for Investment to Cover Income Shortage** ______________ (#4 divided by __%, or the percentage income you can expect to get by investing a lump sum of capital to get a reasonable amount of income. At this point, we use a 6% discount rate.)
6. **Amount of life insurance you would need (1+5)** ______________
7. **Amount of life insurance you now own + liquid investible assets** ______________
8. **Amount of life insurance you need to purchase** ______________ (6 – 7)

Your Taxable Estate

Take out your balance sheet from the first section and start with those assets. We will need to determine just who owns what. Be sure to update for any new assets you have accumulated since you began. Then **delete** from the list any **cash value** from your life insurance policies. **Add** back the actual death benefit from your group insurance and your personal life insurance. Yes, the death benefit, while free from income taxation, is subject to estate taxes along with your other assets. Use the following worksheet to figure out what your taxable estates are. If you are married we need to know what the husband owns, the wife and what is owned jointly. If you are not married, just use one column.

A different type of tax.

ASSETS	HUSBAND	WIFE	JOINT

Now you know the total of the assets in each name and those held jointly. The items held personally are in each of your estates and 50% of the joint assets are in each of your estates. Husbands and wives under most circumstances are able to pass on to each other an unlimited amount of assets without any estate taxes due. This is known as the unlimited marital deduction.

Watch those estate tax laws change!

However, the problem arises upon the second death. In 2002, you could exclude the first million ($1M) of assets from estate tax. Currently, the marginal estate tax rates start at 41% and rise to a maximum rate of 50% for those with a taxable estate of more than $2.5M. Families can shelter a great deal of their assets if they add certain types of trusts to their wills.

For 2004-2005, the exempt amounts rise from $1 million to a $1.5 million exclusion. The exclusion rises to $2 million for 2006-2008 and $3.5M in 2009. Over this time, the highest tax rate drops from 50% to 45%. In 2010, the estate tax will be abolished for one year. In 2011, the exclusion amount drops to $1M and the maximum marginal tax rate will be 60%.

There are various tools you can use to decrease the taxable estate and over the span of this section we will discuss several of the most common ones. As you may know, Congress is looking into ways of eliminating this tax but as of now we are still stuck with it.

In addition, we need to examine state inheritance taxes that can vary from state to state. Probate is another cost that we will deal with later on as well.

How Are Your Assets Titled? 16

One of the features of a coordinated estate plan is having various elements properly working together. This includes having your assets and your wills and trusts set up consistent with the same goals and objectives. In other words, it is essential to have the beneficiaries of your life insurance and retirement plans in sync with the directions of your estate planning documents. *For example, if your will directs all the assets you own to go to your spouse and you designate a nephew as the beneficiary of your life insurance you probably have a problem. Could it be that you did not update the beneficiaries since you wrote the will? Or is it a conscious decision?*

A thorough review of those assets in your retirement and insurance plans will indicate whether you are in agreement with your wills and trusts. It is a good idea that you review these designations at least every 3 to 5 years. Certainly, as you add new assets, it will be important to coordinate the beneficiaries.

The next area that people generally fall short is in the retitling of assets as per trust agreements. For example, if you substitute a revocable living trust (see later sections) for a will, you need to retitle your assets in the name of the trust so that they avoid probate. Any asset left out of the trust will be subject to probate and lose the benefits of the trust you set up. Also, if you have a tax credit trust (explained later) in your will and hope to maximize the benefits of it by having each spouse take advantage of the unified credit, then having all your assets held jointly won't do. Only those assets held individually in each spouse's name could fund those trusts. So, if you have this and forget to split your assets, you will not be able to take advantage of the documents you paid for.

Be sure to review the titling of your assets.

You also need to evaluate the other titles you may be part of to see if it is the most appropriate. If you own property jointly with your children, you may be doing them, as well as yourself, a disservice. Most people do this because they are newly widowed or divorced and think that this is the easiest way for their children to be able to take care of them in the event of an incapacity. *There are other and better ways and we will discuss them later.* In effect, when you put your child's name on your investment you are making a gift of one half of the assets. You probably are exceeding your gift limitations when you do this. In addition, if you do this with capital assets such as stocks, bonds, mutual funds or real estate, you are depriving them of a full **step up** in basis upon your death. Upon death your original basis goes away and the new basis for your heirs is the value on the date of death. Therefore, when you die and they go to sell those assets, they will have your basis on one half and a stepped up basis on the other half, leaving one half of the value to be subject to capital gains tax.

The other issue is that once those assets are titled jointly, half appears to be in control of the children. Not that the children would do anything deceitful, but life happens to all of us. If they are involved in a lawsuit, those joint assets could be tied up in connection with it. In addition, if they were to be a divorce, there could be issues. So, just at a time when you would probably want to help them, you could be having problems yourself. It is wise to reconsider your options here. There are alternatives.

What Happens to Our Money When We Die? 17

When we die, all of our assets go into our "estate". An account needs to be set up to receive all of our assets and the executors of our estate usually do this upon your death. Your executor, having already been designated in your will or revocable living trust, is appointed by the court in the case of a will or automatically in the case of a revocable trust. When you choose someone to be an executor it should be someone familiar with the family finances such as your spouse or one of the children. Hopefully, the person you choose will be familiar with financial issues or seek out the information they need from someone who is.

Your executor can be your spouse, your child, another relative or friend. It is a good idea to name an alternate in case the main person is unable or unwilling to serve at the time needed. A corporate executor is also acceptable such as the trust department of a banking institution. The advantage here is the perpetuity of a corporation.

Distribute your estate according to YOUR wishes.

One of the things one should avoid at all costs is dying *in testate*. What this means is dying without a will or trust to dictate where your assets are to go. When this happens, the state you live in dictates how your assets will be disbursed. For example, in the State of Maryland, if you die without a will and you have a spouse and children, one-half will go to the kids and only one-half to the spouse, even if the children are minors. The spouse has no access to the funds other than to manage it for the children until they come of age. There is a natural progression determined by the state and that progression could be contrary to your wishes. It is also more costly to probate an estate that does not have a will or trust. It is recommended that everyone have a will or revocable trust and that it be reviewed every 3 to 5 years. These documents should be drawn up by an attorney and reviewed by an attorney as well. In addition, if you move out of state after having written one, have it reviewed by an attorney in your new state of residence.

Probate, another cost of transferring your estate, is simply the process of renaming your assets in the heir's names. That process can include lawyer's fees, accountant's fees, appraisals, filing fees, court fees and other miscellaneous expenses. The costs vary from state to state. There are ways of keeping these costs to a minimum and, as we go, we will discuss them.

Once the estate is gathered, appraised and valued, the IRS FORM 706 is completed if the taxable estate exceeds the exemption equivalent. The estate tax is calculated and is then due nine months from date of death. If your estate is not liquid and does not have the available cash to pay the tax, assets must be sold or the funds needed must be borrowed. Examine your balance sheet to see just how much liquidity you have. We will discuss ways to minimize the tax and how to create liquidity later on in this section.

Wills

A will is a legal document detailing the disposition of your estate. It designates an executor and perhaps an alternate, a guardian, if necessary, for your children so that you have the choice, and trustees for trusts set up for the children. Go through the following checklist prior to meeting with your attorney so that you have some of the answers you will need.

_____ Has basic introduction, which identifies testator (you or your spouse).

_____ Includes declaration of domicile for testator.

_____ Includes clause revoking all prior wills and codicils.

_____ Includes declaration of marital status.

_____ Provides for after-born and legally adopted children.

_____ Appoints executor (executrix).

_____ Appoints one or more alternate executors.

_____ Has provision for executor to serve without bond.

_____ Nominates guardian of "persons" of minor children.

_____ Nominates guardian of "estates" of minor children.

_____ Nominates one or more alternate guardians.

_____ Has provision for guardian to serve without bond.

_____ Makes "token" provision for beneficiaries who contest the will.

_____ Provides for Common Disaster (Time Suspension) (Simultaneous Death of _____ days (months.)

_____ Provides for distribution of separate as well as community property (if applicable).

_____ Provides for distribution of estate assets if no family member survives.

_____ Provides for executor (executrix) to operate business without personal liability until estate is closed.

_____ Is dated and has been properly executed by testator.

_____ Has been properly witnessed by two or more persons who have no pecuniary interest in the will (including signatures and addresses.)

Be prepared when you go to see your attorney! It will save you time and money!

Revocable Living Trusts

Will alternative.

As an alternative to a will, one might choose to set up a *revocable living trust.* This trust is funded during your lifetime and governs the assets that have been titled in the name of the trust. Presumably you will want to put all or most of your assets into this trust during your lifetime. During your lifetime you are the beneficiary as well as the trustee. The tax ID used is your social security number. So all income and losses are reported on your personal tax return just as they were before. As trustee, you manage, buy, sell, gift or do anything you wish with your assets just as before the trust's establishment.

Another possible option.

You get to name a successor trustee to take over for you in the event you are incapacitated. This trustee might also serve as your executor administrator of your estate. You can set up tax credit trusts within the document as well as other trusts for children and others. The assets you place in the trust are not subject to probate and pass easily to your heirs. Upon your death, the administrator can gather your assets, value them for estate tax purposes, file your returns for the IRS and your state and distribute the assets presuming the trust has been set up and there are no assets outside of the trust. You also retain privacy for your estate. The revocable living trust in and of itself does NOTHING TO REDUCE ESTATE TAXES. You must include other trust language within it to address this issue.

When you have a revocable living trust your attorney will also prepare a pour-over will, which is short in length but simply states that upon your death if there are any assets found outside the trust, they are to be included with trust assets for the purposes of distribution. Those assets found outside the trust *will* be subject to probate.

As for all estate documents, be sure to consult with an estate-planning attorney.

Tax Credit Trusts

(Also known as Unified Credit Trusts, By-Pass trusts)

Don't let Uncle Sam be a new heir to your estate.

Because everyone can pass on some amount of assets (up to $3,000,000 by the year 2006) estate tax free, one needs to make provisions in a will or revocable living trust so that you do not lose out on this opportunity for your family. If spouses just pass on all their assets to each other with no strings attached, then the first spouse to die loses their right to use the exemption. However, if there is a trust in existence, then the assets in the first spouse's to die name go to fund that trust. The surviving spouse receives income from that trust for his/her lifetime and has some limited access to principal. However, when the second spouse dies, not only do that spouse's assets pass using the exemption amount but the remaining assets in the first spouse's trust pass on estate tax free as well. This means that by 2006, a family will be able to effectively pass on up to $6M estate tax free.

How Our Assets Can Be Passed On 18

Our assets pass on by primarily three methods:

Probate

Probate, as we have learned, is the process by which your assets pass from your estate to your heirs. This process includes the legal aspects, appraisals, accounting fees and other fees that may be incurred to assure the process is complete. The assets pass according to your wishes that are expressed in your will or revocable living trust. If you die in testate, the assets will pass according to the state's law. Usually, if you have a will, the assets covered by the will pass in this fashion. An estate that goes through probate is public and prone to delays.

Pass by Virtue of Law

Certain of your assets pass outside of your wills and trusts. These are those assets to whom you assigned a beneficiary. These include your life insurance policies, annuities, IRAs and other qualified plans. In addition, assets held jointly with your spouse as "joint tenants with rights of survivorship" or "tenants by the entirety." This applies even if you have a revocable living trust. Again, it is wise to review beneficiary designations especially during life cycle events (births, weddings, divorces, deaths) to assure that they are in agreement with your wishes in your legal documents. Beneficiary designations are easy to change once you get the proper forms.

Trusts

There are two basic forms of trusts. One is the revocable living trust (inter vivos), and the other is testamentary (created at death). The Unified Credit Trust as we discussed above is a testamentary trust as it gets funded when the first spouse dies. Assets can flow into a testamentary trust for the benefit of another and not pass directly to the heirs. Most often these trusts are set up for the benefit of a spouse, minor and adult children or when there are special needs.

Set up for the benefit of others.

In the case of special needs, a family with a disabled child might set up a discretionary special needs trust and assign a trustee. This has the effect of protecting assets for that child while still allowing the child to qualify for public benefits.

Estate Shrinkage and How to Minimize It

19

Costs of dying

The high costs of death taxes can shrink your estate dramatically. When you look at the tax rate schedule for the federal estate tax alone, you can readily see how easy it is to reach the 50% tax bracket. Since each person is allowed to pass up to $2,000,000 estate tax free to their heirs, it is vital that to the extent possible, each spouse be able to preserve their rights to pass on this amount individually. This is not possible if what you own is all owned jointly. It may be wise to split the assets so that each spouse has at least up to $2,000,000 in their own names. For most people, this exempts their estate from taxation.

Minimize your taxes upon transfer.

Then, a trust (called a Unified Credit Trust) can be put in your will or revocable living trust that provides for the acceptance of the first $2,000,000 of assets of the first spouse to die. The surviving spouse will receive income from that trust for life and has limited access to principal. However, when the second spouse dies, what is left in that trust or whatever it may have grown to will pass to the children estate tax free in addition to the first $2,000,000 of the second spouse's assets. This way a couple can pass up to $4,000,000 to the children estate tax free. This amount will grow to $3 million dollars each or $6,000,000 for both spouses in the year 2008. Remember, though, in 2011, we revert back to a $675,000 exemption again under current law. Plan to live that long and plan around this. Also, it's worth reminding you that between the equity in your home, life insurance and retirement plans, your estate may be larger than you think – work the numbers!

In addition, if the estate size warrants, a generation skipping transfer trust can be established to provide up to $1,000,000 to the grandchildren estate tax free as well.

Transfer costs

Probate and administrative costs including attorney's fees, accountant's fees and appraisals can serve to shrink an estate. There are several ways to avoid probate. By utilizing a Revocable Living Trust, you can avoid probate on your assets. Jointly held assets avoid probate and so do those assets that pass by beneficiary (annuities, life insurance, pensions). Remember that probate and estate taxes are separate items. While a revocable living trust helps you avoid probate, it does nothing to reduce estate taxes. So you may have to have a unified credit trust added to it or some other form of trust.

Lack of liquidity

If your assets are tied up in illiquid assets, such as real estate or privately held company stock, you may have trouble coming up with enough cash within the nine months from date of death to pay the tax. You will need to sell assets or borrow the necessary funds. This could also apply to a stock portfolio that is going through a market correction nine months after date of death. To sell either type of asset, you might suffer serious losses due to timing and create a "fire sale".

Avoid a "fire sale."

Borrowing only creates a liability for the heirs and a cash flow crunch due to the cost of the interest on the loans. In addition, the estate or the heirs may be unable to borrow at the time.

Therefore, it is logical to try to provide for liquidity in advance of death. One of the best and most cost-effective ways to provide estate liquidity is to purchase life insurance. If you purchase it outside of the estate, the additional liquidity will not serve to increase your estate size. This can be done with the creation of an ***irrevocable trust*** or ***by having the policy owned by your children***. By having this type of trust purchase the insurance for you, you establish an entity that can't be taxed in your estate when you die. Before you let your children own the policy, be sure that you are not causing them to have an estate tax problem. The death benefit of your policy becomes part of their estate.

For a married couple, it is not necessary to purchase two different life insurance policies. They can purchase what is known as a "second to die policy" that insures both under one contract but only pays out upon the second death. But, remember, this trust is ***irrevocable*** so that once it is established, it cannot be revoked or changed. It is a way of prepaying your estate taxes with money that costs pennies on the dollar. If the trustee uses these funds to pay the tax, it leaves the other assets that you have worked so hard for, intact. This is a good technique for larger estates that are not covered by the exemption equivalent, which rises to two million dollars in 2006.

Improper ways of disposing of assets

Many times the wrong heirs inherit the wrong assets. Or the right assets are given to the wrong person. Letting a person who cannot manage money directly receive assets can be a sure way to lose them quickly. In all probability, if a person cannot manage his or her own finances, then the receipt of a large sum will only exacerbate that problem. You can provide for such a person by virtue of a trust that will invest and manage the assets for them and give them income. The trustees can be directed to allow some access to principal upon permission of the trustee. You may want to create some distance between the beneficiary and the trustee by either having a corporate trustee alone or a family member as a co-trustee.

Are your heirs ready to take on their inheritance?

In addition, if you have a child or grandchild with special needs it is advisable that you do not give assets outright to that person. If they are qualified, on their own, to receive state and public benefits, your assets can deprive them of those rights. Therefore, they will have to spend down your assets before they qualify again for their benefits. If you put the assets into a **Discretionary Special Needs Trust,** the assets will be available to them for their comforts in addition to what they are rightly entitled. With proper investment management on the part of the trustee, those assets could last their lifetime. If you are in a situation such as this, be sure all members of the family are aware of the trust so that they do not pass assets directly to the individual.

20 Planning for Incapacity

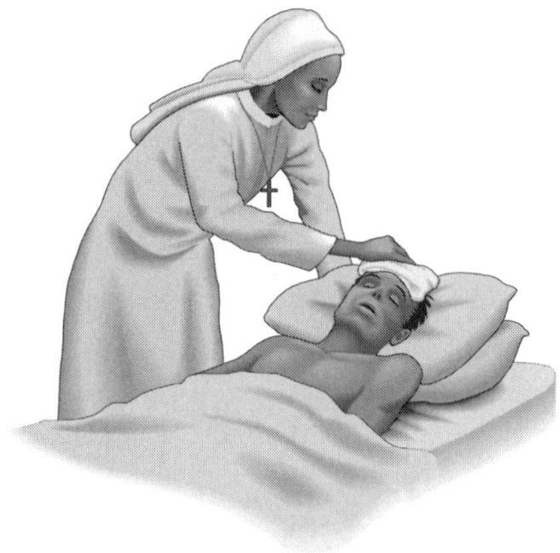

What If You Become Incapacitated?

Becoming incapacitated can happen at any age and due to many reasons. Illness knows no age gap neither do accidents. These issues are appropriate for any family to discuss.

Be prepared.

If you were to become incapacitated and you have not made advance preparations, your family will have to take extraordinary steps to care for you. This can include the need to get a guardianship in order to take care of your finances. That process is a lengthy, painful and costly one. You will need to be declared incompetent under the testimony of three doctors before a judge. Should the judge grant your family the guardianship, they will need to do an annual accounting of your finances to the court, accounting for every penny received and every penny spent down to the stamp to mail the package. This is also very time consuming. There are estate-planning tools that are available, which can provide instructions in the event of these contingencies. These tools are referred to as '"advance directives."

Durable Power of Attorney

Designate someone to take over if you are incapacitated.

This short document, also prepared by your attorney, allows someone you designate to step in on your behalf and take care of your finances in the event you become incapacitated. If you have a will as your main estate disposition document, then you should discuss setting this up with your attorney as well. It allows them to write checks from your account, buy and sell assets, borrow on your behalf and manage your business affairs. Just because you may be married and own your assets jointly you shouldn't assume you are okay.

Most joint assets need two signatures to authorize transactions. So you need this too. It only comes into play if you are incapacitated and you set the rules. You may have your doctor or more than one sign off as to your lack of ability to tend your own affairs or any other formula you decide. This document will need to be signed and notarized when it is prepared while you are well. We recommend that it is good to have this reaffirmed every 5 or so years just to keep the signature current while you are healthy.

Keep these important documents up to date.

Revocable Living Trust

If you have a revocable living trust you will have a successor trustee to yourself and that person will step in on your behalf in the event of your incapacity. You do not need a separate durable power of attorney in that event. Your successor trustee in a properly drafted document has all the powers necessary to be able to act on your behalf.

Health Care Power of Attorney

This document as prepared by your attorney gives someone the authority to act on your behalf to make medical decisions if you can't. This is important to have in place so that surgical procedures and other treatments can occur if you are unable to make those decisions yourself due to an incapacity. A copy of this signed agreement should go to the person you assigned with the powers and another to your primary physician.

Living Will

This document, again to be prepared by your attorney, addresses life support and heroics in the event you should ever be in need of this. This is a personal decision but it is important to let people know your wishes. It relieves the family of some heavy-duty decision-making. Again, a copy should be with your personal representative and/or your doctor.

Long Term Care

See earlier sections relative to this topic.

21 Gifting

Basic Rules

Gift well, gift often, but gift properly!

Anyone can gift to anyone else up to $11,000 per year indexed for inflation. A husband and wife can gift $11,000 each for a total of $22,000 to each child, in-law, grandchild or other person. It is advised to write separate checks from two different accounts in the event the IRS questions the gift. We also recommend that to avoid a situation where it could appear that two gifts were made in the same year, avoid giving 'holiday' gifts close to the end of the year. The gift checks should clear before December 31 of any given year. All too often, someone receives a gift at Christmas and is so busy that they may not make it to the bank till later that week. If you wait too many days, the check will not clear the bank until the next calendar year. Then if you repeat the gift again, it could cause it to appear like two gifts in the same year. So it is a good idea to gift early to assure that you avoid this potential problem. You can gift more than the allowed gift but there are tax consequences. You either need to file a gift tax return and pay tax for the excess over the $11,000 or you can file a return and chip away at your unified credit leaving less available at your death.

Gift Expansion Techniques

There are two techniques that work especially well for parents and grandparents. The first technique to be able to expand a gift to a child or grandchild is to pay directly for medical and/or tuition costs. In other words, if a check is written directly to the medical care provider or a school, the amounts do not matter. In addition, then, a gift can be made directly to that same recipient for up to the $11,000 per person limitation. Given the costs of medical care and private school or colleges these days, a substantial gifting scenario may be presented.

A grandparent's dream.

The second technique involves the use of life insurance. We can look at two scenarios. One is the parent or grandparent that only has $11,000 or less to gift but has several children or grandchildren. Rather than giving one or two thousand dollars to each, the $11,000 can pay the premium on a life insurance policy with each child and or grandchild proportional beneficiaries. A trust can be set up for this if you wanted. In this way, not only are the earnings on the cash build up tax deferred, the cash is available and liquid. The biggest feature here is that the $11,000 gift could be multiplied several fold by the death benefit provided. So now, there is a greater impact on each child and/or grandchild for each dollar received.

Make those dollars that you gift count!

The same can be accomplished within the situation where the parents and/or grandparents can afford up to the full amount each year to each child/grandchild. All or a portion of the gift can apply to an insurance policy and therefore expand what you make available for the children. This allows for additional flexibility for the parent or grandparent to spend additional assets or do charitable gifting without depriving the heirs of the family assets.

Charitable Gifts

Now we will talk about your social funds. This is the amount of money that you donate to organizations to help make other lives better. First of all, if you donate money or assets to a bona fide charity you can deduct amounts up to 50% of your income in any one year. Amounts that you donate that exceed that amount are carried forward to future years. Amounts that you give to any one organization that exceed $250 require you to have a receipt in the event you are audited. For some organizations there are other limitations for the deductibility of contributions. Check with your tax advisor. You may also deduct for your mileage that you put on your car as you perform activities relative to the charity.

Your social funds.

Donations to charitable organizations can be made several ways. One, of course, is cash. The other is by donating assets that you may own including real estate, stocks, bonds and other personal or investment property. You will get a current deduction for the fair market value on the date of the gift not just your original purchase price. You can change the beneficiary of your insurance to your favorite organization or more than one and/or change the owner to the charity, and then you can deduct the premiums. In that way, you can magnify the effects of your donated dollars.

Many choices.

Tax Planning, Retirement Income Planning and Your Charitable Contributions

Many people have investments such as stocks that they have owned for a while with a very low basis. To sell them would bring on large amounts of capital gains and a large tax liability. Yet, to keep the shares may not allow you to get sufficient income from this part of your portfolio. If you fall into this category we may have a solution. Why not set up a charitable remainder trust? Donate the appreciated property into the trust. The charity who is the beneficiary of this trust would sell it, reinvest the proceeds for income, pass on an income stream to you and your spouse for your lifetime and you totally avoid having to pay the capital gains tax. In addition, you get a tax deduction for the fair market value of the investment you contributed. In this way, you get the benefit of a higher income stream from the full value without having to lose value to tax payments. Upon your death, the value in the trust goes to the charity or charities you have chosen. This has the effect of lowering your taxable estate. Many people then set up an **irrevocable trust** to purchase life insurance on their lives. They use the tax savings from the donation to help pay the premiums. In that way, they replace the asset value for their heirs and yet keep it out of their estates.

Donating assets can be good for you.

Charitable Remainder Trusts/ Wealth Replacement

Highlights of how it works:

- Gift an appreciated asset to charity in a trust
- The charity sells the asset but neither the donor nor the charity has to pay capital gains tax
- The charity reinvests the proceeds and provides income to the donor and spouse during their lifetime
- Donor gets to deduct the appreciated value of the asset on the income tax return
- Upon the second spouse's death, the corpus of the trust goes to the charity
- The donor can replace the asset for the children by setting up a wealth replacement trust upon donation
- The wealth replacement trust is irrevocable and owns a life insurance policy on the donor.
- The death benefit remains outside the donor's estate because of the nature of the trust
- When the donor dies, the children become the beneficiaries of the insurance, *income and estate tax free.*

There are other techniques used in this area of planning and should be taken up with a qualified planner or attorney who work in this area. This is only one example of a commonly used technique. However, since various family needs are different, other types of arrangements can be put together that can meet them.

Part Three Summary

I hope you have found that this section helps to round out your financial planning. You should take the time to review your benefit plans at work and consult with your benefit office to get a better handle on this. Then consult with your financial advisor to be sure your risk management plan is in place. Apply for any additional insurances that may be necessary but also review your homeowner's, rental and car insurances also. There could be gaps there, as well. Consult your insurance agent.

Kudos! You have done a spectacular job.

Be sure to fully discuss with an attorney all your estate planning needs. Have that estate planning attorney put the proper documents in place. Be sure to check out the attorney you choose, just as you checked out your financial advisor. Get recommendations and then check them out with your local chapter of the Bar Association.

Once you have implemented these areas, you can focus on your organization and investments once again.

Epilogue

Now you know how all the parts fit together to form a cohesive plan for your financial future. It is necessary to complete all three parts of this book and then revisit them again regularly. We recommend that the investment portfolio be reviewed at least quarterly and the estate area every year or two or as soon as a lifecycle event occurs. By this we mean a marriage, a birth, a death, or a divorce. As far as the estate section is concerned your attorney should initiate a review every two or three years.

Keep this book handy!

As you can appreciate now, a change in one area really affects the whole. You are well prepared to begin taking control. You should constantly try to learn more about each area and go back to the exercises, as you may need to do new projections. More information is available and you should investigate subscribing to those journals and newsletters that will keep you informed. There are classes you can enroll in through your Adult Education programs through your local school systems. There are also college level courses that you might want to embark upon to gain more knowledge.

Whatever way you choose to learn is good. Just don't ever become complacent and feel you know enough. None of us has that luxury and just as professionals need to take continuing education courses, so should you. Please feel free to let us know if you want to receive our free quarterly newsletter, *The Advisor*, or visit our website www.fishmanfinancial.com. There will always be more information provided there.

Good luck reaching your goals!

A Appendix: Daily Budget Worksheet

The Daily Budget Worksheet we talked about in Part 1 is on the facing page. Feel free to copy this page, make it larger or reproduce it on computer. Refer to it daily while you are monitoring your expenses. Also, if you and your spouse, significant other or partner are working with you, use two copies but combine them at month's end for worksheets in Appendix B.

DAILY SPENDING	1	2	3	4	5	6	7	8	9	10	11	12	13	14	15	16	17	18	19	20	21	22	23	24	25	26	27	28	29	30	31	TOTALS
Groceries																																
Eat Out																																
Gas Bill																																
Electric Bill																																
Telephone Bill																																
Long Distance																																
Cell Phone Bill																																
Cleaners																																
Hair Cut/Products																																
Drug Store																																
Household Purchases																																
Gas																																
Car Repair																																
Transportation (train, bus)																																
Entertainment																																
Newspaper/Magazine																																
Snacks																																
Club Dues																																
Vacation/Camps																																
Domestic Help																																
Child Care																																
Subscriptions																																
Books																																
Gifts																																
Medical (nonreimbursed)																																
Life Insurance																																
Health Insurance																																
Other Insurance																																
Alimony																																
Child Support																																
Savings																																
Charity																																
Accounting/Legal																																
Education																																
Tax Payments																																
Pension Contributions																																
Miscellaneous/Other																																

B Appendix: Monthly Budget Worksheet

Transfer information from Appendix A to the forms on the following pages. Reprioritize what you want to spend next month and put that amount in next month's Budget column. Start a new daily sheet. When you enter the Actual at the end of the month, you will see just how successful you have been in controlling your cash outlays.

Monthly Budget vs. Actual

	JANUARY		FEBRUARY		MARCH	
	Budget	Actual	Budget	Actual	Budget	Actual
Groceries						
Eat Out						
Gas Bill						
Electric Bill						
Telephone Bill						
Long Distance						
Cell Phone Bill						
Cleaners						
Hair Cut/Products						
Drug Store						
Household Purchases						
Gas						
Car Repair						
Transportation						
Entertainment						
Newspaper/Magazine						
Snacks						
Club Dues						
Vacation/Camps						
Domestic Help						
Child Care						
Subscriptions						
Books						
Gifts						
Medical (nonreimbursed)						
Life Insurance						
Health Insurance						
Other Insurance						
Alimony						
Child Support						
Savings						
Charity						
Accounting/Legal						
Education						
Tax Payments						
Pension Contributions						
Miscellaneous/Other						

Monthly Budget vs. Actual

	APRIL		MAY		JUNE	
	Budget	Actual	Budget	Actual	Budget	Actual
Groceries						
Eat Out						
Gas Bill						
Electric Bill						
Telephone Bill						
Long Distance						
Cell Phone Bill						
Cleaners						
Hair Cut/Products						
Drug Store						
Household Purchases						
Gas						
Car Repair						
Transportation						
Entertainment						
Newspaper/Magazine						
Snacks						
Club Dues						
Vacation/Camps						
Domestic Help						
Child Care						
Subscriptions						
Books						
Gifts						
Medical (nonreimbursed)						
Life Insurance						
Health Insurance						
Other Insurance						
Alimony						
Child Support						
Savings						
Charity						
Accounting/Legal						
Education						
Tax Payments						
Pension Contributions						
Miscellaneous/Other						

Monthly Budget vs. Actual

	JULY		AUGUST		SEPTEMBER	
	Budget	Actual	Budget	Actual	Budget	Actual
Groceries						
Eat Out						
Gas Bill						
Electric Bill						
Telephone Bill						
Long Distance						
Cell Phone Bill						
Cleaners						
Hair Cut/Products						
Drug Store						
Household Purchases						
Gas						
Car Repair						
Transportation						
Entertainment						
Newspaper/Magazine						
Snacks						
Club Dues						
Vacation/Camps						
Domestic Help						
Child Care						
Subscriptions						
Books						
Gifts						
Medical (nonreimbursed)						
Life Insurance						
Health Insurance						
Other Insurance						
Alimony						
Child Support						
Savings						
Charity						
Accounting/Legal						
Education						
Tax Payments						
Pension Contributions						
Miscellaneous/Other						

Monthly Budget vs. Actual

	OCTOBER		NOVEMBER		DECEMBER	
	Budget	Actual	Budget	Actual	Budget	Actual
Groceries						
Eat Out						
Gas Bill						
Electric Bill						
Telephone Bill						
Long Distance						
Cell Phone Bill						
Cleaners						
Hair Cut/Products						
Drug Store						
Household Purchases						
Gas						
Car Repair						
Transportation						
Entertainment						
Newspaper/Magazine						
Snacks						
Club Dues						
Vacation/Camps						
Domestic Help						
Child Care						
Subscriptions						
Books						
Gifts						
Medical (nonreimbursed)						
Life Insurance						
Health Insurance						
Other Insurance						
Alimony						
Child Support						
Savings						
Charity						
Accounting/Legal						
Education						
Tax Payments						
Pension Contributions						
Miscellaneous/Other						

Glossary

Activities of Daily Living – Those activities that include dressing, toileting, grooming, transporting and bathing. It is the inability to perform several of these functions that can make you eligible to make a claim on your long-term care policy.

Actual – As it refers to the budget it is the dollars spent on purchases of goods and services.

ADV – This is the form that a financial planner who charges fees for their services must file with either the Securities and Exchange Commission and/or the state where they practice. It is a full disclosure as to that advisor's education, practice guidelines, past experience and how they operate their business including the fees they charge. This document must also disclose any disciplinary actions against the advisor. An advisor must offer you a copy of this document prior to your doing business with them. In addition, they must offer you an updated copy annually.

Annuities – These are investment vehicles put out by insurance companies that can either have a fixed rate of return or a variable rate of return. The income is tax deferred on both.

Balance Sheet – A snapshot of your assets and liabilities on any given date.

Beneficiary – The designation you give to your annuities, life insurance and retirement plans for the recipient of their respective values when you die. Those assets that pass by beneficiary designation do not go through probate.

Benefit Period – The length of time during which you will receive benefits from disability insurance or long-term care insurance.

Capital Gain or Loss – This is the current value minus the basis. If you have owned the asset for less than 12 months, the gain or loss is short term and any gain is taxed at regular rates. If you have owned the investment for over 12 months the gain or loss is long term. Long-term gains are taxed at a maximum of 15% and less depending on your income.

Capital Gains Distributions – Usually these are distributions made to shareholders of a mutual fund and are pro rata shares of the capital gains the mutual fund has incurred over the year by normal trades as well as those trades triggered by liquidations by shareholders.

Certificate of Deposit – Offered by banks, it is a savings vehicle with a fixed holding period and usually with a fixed income during that holding period. Usually you cannot get out of it prior to the end of the holding period without a surrender penalty. The interest is fully taxable as earned unless it is held in a retirement account.

CFP (Certified Financial Planner) – One of the education credentials to look for in a financial planner.

ChFC (Chartered Financial Consultant) – An alternative educational credential similar to the CFP that a financial planner might hold.

COLA – Cost of living adjustment, usually a rider on certain insurances to assure that your benefit will go up over time to keep up with inflation.

Commissions – Earnings that a planner may earn from the sale of an investment product. It is usually set by the investment you put your money in. (i.e. mutual funds, limited partnerships)

Compound Interest – Interest earned on an ever-growing balance due to the balance being increased every period by the interest earned (can be daily, monthly, etc.).

Cost Basis – This is the "tax" cost of an asset. For a mutual fund it is the original purchase price plus any new purchases plus any dividends and capital gains reinvestments. For real estate it is the original purchase price plus the costs of any improvements. For investment real estate it is the original purchase price plus the costs of any improvements minus accumulated depreciation.

Coupon – The stated interest on a bond.

Creditor – A person or company to whom you owe money.

Depreciation – The process of writing off as an expense the cost of a capital asset over its useful life.

Dividends – Distributions from corporations based on profits. They are taxable at 15%.

Dollar Cost Averaging – The disciplined process of investing by purchasing a fixed dollar amount of a fund, stock or bond every month.

Durable Power of Attorney – A document that comes into play after you incur a disabling illness or accident that allows someone to act on your behalf financially.

Escrowed Funds – Money put aside for a later use.

Executor – The person named by you in your will or trust that will carry out your wishes according to your will when you die.

Financial Planning Process – This is the process of gathering information from a client including facts, goals, hopes and dreams and the analysis of that information as to current scenario and future projections.

Goals – End results you are looking for so that you can formulate financial strategies. Can be short term, intermediate or long term.

Growth – Investments with the primary objective to increase in value in either a short or more extended period of time.

Independent Financial Advisor – An advisor that works for themselves rather than an employee of a larger company that has proprietary products to sell.

Inflation – A rise in the cost of living that is evidenced by an oversupply of money, rising prices and interest rates, short supply of production, and increased pressure on wage hikes and cost of housing.

IRA – Individual Retirement Plan allowing for an annual contribution up to $2,000 or earnings whichever is less.

Irrevocable Trust – A trust document that once set up cannot be changed.

Joint Tenants Rights of Survivorship – Joint ownership that allows the surviving owner to own the asset outright.

Liquidity – The degree to which an investment can be easily sold or traded in for cash at a value equal to initial investment with no fluctuation in value.

Ordinary Income – Income that is taxed at your tax bracket and includes wages, business income, interest, rental income, pensions, etc.

Passive Income – Income from an investment where you do not take an active role in management.

Probate – The process by which your assets change title upon your death.

Purchasing Power – What amount of money it takes to purchase a set amount of goods and/or services.

Recession – A period in the business cycle evidenced by peaked interest rates, tight money, rising unemployment, sluggish growth and a drop in the investment markets.

Recovery – The period in the business cycle following a recession with lowering interest rates, rising productivity, a rise in bond prices, and lower unemployment.

Required Minimum Distribution – This is the amount one must start withdrawing from traditional IRA's and other retirement plans at age 70½. Tables put together by the IRS set this amount and all distributions are fully taxable as ordinary income.

Revocable Living Trust – A trust that is set up and can take the place of a will. Assets held in this trust during your lifetime pass on without probate. This document can be changed or terminated at the will of the trustee. Usually a pour-over will should be in place as well to catch any assets outside of the trust upon death and then put them into the trust for distribution purposes. Assets outside of the trust are subject to probate. These trusts by themselves do nothing to reduce estate taxes.

Tangibles – These are investments in real property, equipment and other capital assets.

Tax Credits – Some investments allow the taxpayer to take a credit on their tax return after their final tax is calculated. That simply means that the amount of the credit is subtracted from the actual tax liability directly reducing it dollar for dollar.

Tax Deductions – Items that you can use on your tax return to reduce taxable income. These include business expenses and itemized deductions, if you are eligible, among others.

Tax Deferred – Investment vehicles that allow earnings to not be taxed in the immediate but rather will accumulate and be taxed at a later date upon withdrawal from that vehicle. These can include IRA's, Pension Plans including 401k's, annuities, and insurance.

Total Return – The returns on an investment taking into account the income and changes in value. For example, an investment with a 8% dividend that falls by 3% in value gives the investor a 5% total return.

Unlimited Marital Deduction – Spouses can pass an infinite amount of assets to each other upon death without incurring estate taxes.

Volatility – The swings in the price of an investment, sometimes called "beta". The higher the value of "beta" the higher the volatility.

Index

U

V

W

About the Author

Photo by Danny Peck of PeckStudios.net

LOIS FISHMAN

Lois Fishman, a Certified Financial Planner, has been educating people about their finances since 1976, when she started a firm to prepare tax returns. She expanded her practice to include tax planning and then to comprehensive financial planning. Her desire to work with people and help them prepare for retirement led her to develop a financial planning practice in 1983, now known as Fishman Financial Services. She specializes in retirement and estate planning for individuals and families.

Lois speaks regularly to pre- and post-retirees and works with many organizations in Montgomery County, Maryland. She is a frequent speaker at many of the senior centers, NARFE (National Association of Retired Federal Employees) and various support groups for widows. She has been the host of a radio show dealing with financial issues on WMET and has been a guest on CNBC (*Money Matters*), DC Channel 20, and Montgomery Cable Channel 21.

She is active in her community. As a Leadership Montgomery Graduate (1998), she has participated in many community activities, including the Montgomery County Business Roundtable for Education, and the Montgomery County Chamber of Commerce, among others.

She is the chair of the Board of Governors for Chelsea School in Silver Spring, Maryland, a private school dedicated to students with language-based learning differences.

Lois lives in Rockville, Maryland, with her husband and her dog and is the mother of two grown children, Susan and David.